POSITIVE THINKING

DISCOVER THE MAGIC OF POSITIVE THINKING AND HOW TO ACHIEVE YOUR GOALS AND SUCCEED IN LIFE

STOP NEGATIVE THINKING AND RELIEVE STRESS NOW

THE SECRET OF YOUR SUCCESS LIES WITHIN YOUR MIND

FRANK MULLANI

Copyright, Legal Notice and Disclaimer:

This publication is protected under the US Copyright Act of 1976 and all other applicable international, federal, state and local laws, and all rights are reserved, including resale rights: you are not allowed to give or sell this Guide to anyone else.

Please note that much of this publication is based on research, personal experience and anecdotal evidence. Although the author and publisher have made every reasonable attempt to achieve complete accuracy of the content in this Guide, they assume no responsibility for errors or omissions. Also, you should use this information as you see fit, and at your own risk. Your particular situation may not be exactly suited to the examples illustrated here; in fact, it's likely that they won't be the same, and you should adjust your use of the information and recommendations accordingly.

Any trademarks, service marks, product names or named features are assumed to be the property of their respective owners, and are used only for reference. There is no implied endorsement if we use one of these terms.

Finally, use your head. Nothing in this Guide is intended to replace common sense, legal, medical or other professional advice, and is meant to inform and entertain the reader. So have fun with this complete **POSITIVE THINKING** guide.

Copyright © 2013 Frank Mullani. All rights reserved worldwide.

Table of Content:

- How This Book Can Help You? ---------------Page 10
- Why You Need to be a Positive Thinker and Why You Need This Book? ---------------------------Page 12
- Training The Subconscious Mind for Self-Improvement -------------------------------------- Page 15
- There Is a Winner in Each One of Us, Discover How to Feed the Winner Mindset and Advance toward Your Goals with the Help of Positive Thinking ---Page 23
- The Subconscious Mind and Positive Thinking ---Page 29
- The Relationship between Positive Thinking and the Law of Attraction --------------------------------Page 40
- Overcoming Negative Thoughts to Move Forward in Life --Page 55
- How to Set Goals to Achieve Everything You Want in Life --Page 61
- More on How to Set Goals ---------------------Page 67
- How to Attract Abundance Through Positive Thinking ---Page 76
- How to Improve Your Self-Esteem and Become a Positive Thinker ----------------------------------Page 84
- A Guide on How to Eliminate Negative Thinking, Stress and Fear ---------------------------------Page 93
- Discover the 10 Laws to Unleash the Power of Positive Thinking ---------------------------------Page 101

- How to Relieve Stress to Advance With Your Life Goals --Page 111
- Positive Thinking and Success - Changing Your Life through the Magic of Positive Thinking --Page 115
- POSITIVE THINKING IMAGES TO INSPIRE YOU --Page 119
- Positive Thinking and Motivational Quotes to Keep You Inspired --Page 124
- Having a Positive Thinking Mind – How it can Benefit You? --------------------------------------Page 128
- How to Eliminate Your Mental Blocks to Attain Success and be Positive--------------------Page 135
- Conclusion --Page 140
- About the Author-----------------------------------Page 143

How This Book Can Help You:

This book will help you transform your life and accomplish everything you desire with courage and determination. With easy to follow yet very powerful principles described in this book you will awake the power inside you and unleash the magic of positive thinking in your favor so you eliminate negative thoughts and stress while you accomplish all your dreams.

I wrote this book with the profound conviction that all we want in life is possible through the magic of positive thinking. All we need to follow are proven guidelines and constructive steps that will make us succeed in life. You will find all these guidelines and these steps in this book so you can start right now with the positive transformation of your life. I've been defeated many times in life but I consider myself a very successful person because despite all the adversity I've faced in the past one thing remains intact and that is my positive thinking attitude. I achieved many of my goals in the past and started from scratch but life gave me some unexpected surprises that let me with nothing but my own self and I had to start all over again. Today I am back on my fit and on track to achieving new dreams and new goals and this is thanks to one of my most valuable assets, my indestructible positive thinking mind. My goal with this book is to help you overcome any negative thoughts that you may have and to plant the seed for a better you with the steps and techniques revealed in this book through the magic of positive thinking.

Thank you for reading my book,

Frank Mullani

Why You Need to be a Positive Thinker and Why You Need This Book?

Thinking positively is not something you embrace unless you have a strong desire to succeed in life. A positive mindset is at the root of every major human achievement and at the core of every truly successful person. Optimism is the seed that helps your dreams become a reality and the main energy that attracts a myriad of benefits to your life. By thinking positively you will not only affect your life in a constructive and encouraging way, you will overcome depression, relieve stress, eliminate anxiety and even strengthen your overall health.

A positive attitude and a positive mindset are the best natural remedies for your frustrations and fears when you learn how to unleash the power that lies inside you and discover the magic of positive thinking. It is undeniable that positive thinking has a beneficial effect in your life and in fact numerous studies have shown that a positive attitude makes a person stronger and with a stronger health condition than those who have pessimistic thoughts. It is all about the energy you project and how you are able to direct all this power to conquer your goals.

With this book you will learn how to develop a positive and enduring winning attitude. Optimism attracts good things into your life naturally and if you develop this attitude you will certainly conquer all your dreams and be surrounded by a field of magnetic positive energy that will bring even more good to your existence.

Attaining this attitude requires practice and persistence and the right steps to learn how to set your goals and this is precisely what you will learn with this book, how to be positive and achieve whatever you want in life from now. Stop worrying about everything and start facing your life with new energy and a new resolution from now on, that is the goal of my book and I hope I can transmit that to you through the following chapters. You are what you think you are and you deserve what you think you deserve so start thinking abundantly and with optimism about your life from now on.

Start using positive affirmations from now and believe in your inner strength and energy, it is all inside you, you just have to let it manifest to start attracting all that you deserve. You are the one who can create your path, your reality and not the other way around. Life is all about on which side you decide to be, on the winning and positive side or on the negative and losing side. You are in control, and yes you can do it! Life is too short to be trapped into our own psychological mind made prison, you have to overcome your own demons and start living the life you want and deserve now and you can do this through the magic of positive thinking revealed in this book. Get all the resources you need to change your life now with this book and start receiving all the power of positive thinking now!

TRAINING THE SUBCONSCIOUS MIND FOR SELF-IMPROVEMENT

Understanding the Subconscious State of Mind

As human beings, we all think. And we don't just think, we tend to think a lot. So much so, that more than half the time, we don't even remember a lot of the things that have crossed our minds.

According to figures from UCLA, any normal human being has about 70,000 thoughts a day. This could also be translated as 48.61 thoughts per minute.

Imagine the amount of thinking one does in a day. Now close your eyes and think hard; do you remember all that you thought of about an hour ago? Probably you just remember a small portion of your thoughts. The reason is that we tend to receive a number of inputs in the form of stimuli, a range of thoughts that cross our mind, but our brain does not actively register them. These thoughts are said to be subconscious thoughts.

Subconscious describes something which is below our awareness level. For example, you go for an interview and there are a number of candidates sitting there. You look at all of them, but may not talk to them all. But, somewhere in the subconscious mind, all of the faces are registered. A few days later you see a person in a mall who looks familiar. You keep on tapping your mind trying to place the person. Depending on how strongly you have registered the face, you may remember this person as one of the candidates at the interview.

The Need to Train the Subconscious Mind

The need to train the subconscious mind does not arise in everyone. It only arises in people who realize the power of the subconscious mind.

Negative Beliefs: The subconscious mind is a huge storehouse of information, knowledge, and beliefs. Our beliefs that we have secured in our childhood have been so deeply ingrained that they become a part of our personality and reflect in our behavior. Even if we try to change things at the conscious level, the deep down beliefs will be a hindrance. So, it becomes necessary to change things at the subconscious level. It would be like changing the programming of your computer so you can run the same applications more efficiently.

So, in order to change the negative beliefs about yourself, it is important to **change the subconscious programming**. For some people this can be a way to attain success in life also and it definitely is once you start exchanging your negative beliefs for positive ones.

Distractions: Distractions are a major hindrance when it comes to success in life. These distractions also come from the 70,000 thoughts that arise in our mind every day. If a person is able to control the direction of these thoughts, success will not be so far away. This is where focus comes into play. You have to focus your mind into attainable short-term positive goals and thoughts, so you start walking into the path of positive outcomes. Managing your thoughts on a conscious level is a must if you want to achieve your goals.

Control of Subconscious Thoughts Over Mind

Another reason is that our conscious thoughts are always driven by our subconscious thoughts. If you think you are not well prepared and may not do well in an exam or a job interview, your performance is likely to go down as your subconscious mind has already registered your insecurity.

Subconscious thoughts win in case of conflict: It is important to **train the subconscious mind,** as in times of conflict the subconscious mind always prevails over the conscious. For example, if you are Acrophobic (fear of heights), chances are that every time you have to travel by plane, that fear will always cross your mind, despite all your conscious efforts.

Therefore, our subconscious mind becomes a password to most of the information and impressions that we might have to react to at different stages and situations in life. Consequently, there is a need to train our subconscious thoughts.

Improving and Training our Subconscious Thoughts

While a lot of people lose focus while running after their goals, they don't realize it and try to look for reasons elsewhere for the causes of their failure. They don't realize that the answer lies within them.

There are a number of ways of to achieve self-improvement and focus:

1. Writing down your thoughts - Choose a time and write whatever comes to your mind during 10 minutes. You might find it difficult initially, but over a period of time it becomes easy and you attain better control both you're your thoughts and writing. Also, when you write down your thoughts, it becomes easier to set your goals so you can achieve every one of these objectives and mark it with a check sign as you do with a "to do list."

2. Meditation - Meditation holds great importance in the training of your mind. It helps achieve better focus; it improves concentration that also leads to a gain in

cognitive power. When you meditate your brain becomes more receptive to new ideas. Meditation also manages helping you achieve clarity. When you are meditating do so with relaxing music that feeds your spirit and makes you feel at peace. This way your conscious mind will be more likely to engage in positive affirmations and in setting positive goals as you will be creating a state of calm and constructive visualization where repeating affirmations will reprogram your brain. Meditation is defined as a concentrated and focused attention on a thought to reach a state of full concentration and mental relaxation. Focus your mind on positive topics, sounds and images that nourish your inner spirit and your subconscious mind.

3. Analytics and Problem solving – by using the subconscious state of mind to solve problems we develop the skill of sharpening the powers of our minds. Think of a problem. Undertake the puzzle to solve it. Make different hypothesis and mull over the problem for a few days. The solution will come to you as you keep on thinking about it. This will hone your analytical skills, which also will work as life skills for many people.

4. Visualization: This is a very important tool for people who wish success in life. Visualizing one's goal constantly, thinking of the ways and means of achieving it,

will slowly affect the subconscious mind and it will start to accept that idea and it will become a part of your reality. Visualizing images has a very powerful effect on our minds. They are able to reprogram our brains for good or bad. It all depends on what type of images you feed your brain. Even colors have an effect on the mood of a person so much that you can expose yourself to inspiring images that are in relation to your lifetime goals to reprogram your subconscious mind by absorbing this new visual information through repeated exposure to these images.

Get a clear picture in your mind of what you want to achieve, even if it does not exist in the present you will have it programmed into your subconscious. Then you can begin to search for steps to achieve it, and you will start to identify the steps needed to make this image a reality even though it does not exist yet. For example, Steve Jobs had a clear picture of what he wanted with his smart phone idea; it was inside his mind before becoming a reality. Visualizing is not just about focusing on the end goal or result; it also involves the process where you imagine the steps you need to go through to achieve it. It is about envisioning the different phases required to get to what you've visualized inside your mind as if you were watching a movie before it happens, so that it becomes a reality.

5. Conscious effort – Despite the fact that a lot of people might disagree, no one can dispute the power of a conscious and concentrated effort. Someway, somewhere you will be able to break your current pattern and move towards a path of self-improvement and reaching your goals through a systematic conscious effort of filtering your thoughts.

6. Emulate successful people – try to emulate the positive aspects of the lives of successful people. Learn about their achievements and their failures and why they became successful. Chances are that through the power of persistence and positive thinking they attained their goals in life, so you can do it too. Try to learn about other successful people´s experiences so you encourage yourself to keep on trying.

It has often been observed that a lot of people have stopped following their goals, because they have begun to believe that they do not have time to achieve them. If you do not find your goals worth your time, then are these goals really worth being followed? Focus on small achievable goals first and start building your success from there on. Or are you still not able to determine the path you need to take? It is not about spending hours meditating or going for brainstorming sessions with likeminded people; it is about taking small steps at a time; one can think while driving, while walking, while performing any activity in life. You need to filter the clutter of thoughts that cross through your mind and focus on the ones that will bring your closer to your goals. With this approach in mind the path to success will become clearer and more attainable.

There Is a Winner in Each One of Us. Discover How to Feed the Winner Mindset and Advance toward Your Goals with the Help of Positive Thinking

Within each one of us there is a successful person who is just waiting for an opportunity to show up. Deep inside every one of us there is that great desire to succeed and overcome any adversity. The psychological fear is the enemy that does not allow this wish to become a reality. Each human being has strengths and weaknesses, but those who overcome their weaknesses and cultivate their strengths are the ones that really advance in life.

Nobody is perfect or invincible. We must focus on cultivating our winning thoughts and overcoming our defeats and surpassing the cowardice. The person who doesn't take risks for fear of failure is destined to a permanent stagnation that will not allow him to discover the true powers of his inner greatness. Although we are not all the same, all human beings dream of something better, with a better life, to find a purpose for our existence and build our inner being.

One way to feed the winner inside us is by cultivating good habits. The adoption of common practices focusing on short-term achievable goals is a method that builds and forms the foundations to become a real leader. More than a routine, habits tend to become either fundamentals for success or for failure. So the focus should be on promoting good habits that are defined once we have identified a purpose and defined our short term goals.

We address each one of these short-term goals with mental clarity and a truly positive and constructive attitude. Fear of failure must completely be set aside, things as simple as completing a report or getting into the habit of exercising daily are able to raise our self-esteem and have a very powerful effect in building a positive mindset. The systematic postponement of our goals causes the triumph of the loser over the winner. By adopting the habit of constructive routines, we are able to overcome procrastination.

We can program our mind by looking at positive images that inspire a winning attitude and a positive approach towards life. We can learn something new every day. The thirst for continuous learning must be a determined purpose to gradually nourish our knowledge. More knowledge equals more strength while building our self-esteem and our intellect at the same time. An individual with knowledge is a winner full of confidence. Learning new skills is great nourishment for your mind and is definitely a way to set the foundations towards new goals in life. Humans learn by imitation and repetition so it is ideal to adopt routines that are based on proven and successful models and to emulate them and make these routines daily habits to which we shall be making our own variations with creativity.

Always be observant and analytical; never lose the curiosity to know more and read as much as possible about what you're passionate about. We live in the age of knowledge where you can access a myriad of information all the time in various formats and almost constantly we are able build our own wisdom and thrive. The one who is constantly learning is the one who gets the edge, moves forward and is always positive. Set a goal to learn something new each week so it can bring you closer and closer to your objectives. This will certainly help you stay focused and achieve incremental successes that will build an even stronger positive attitude.

Do not settle; life can give you as much as you ask and as much as you want to get. Success and wealth belong to the one that tirelessly is seeking a better life. Keep your focus, give priority to what you know works for you, what has proven successful outcomes and always evaluate and refine your strategies. The most successful people don't go shooting darts in all directions, generally they focus on a winning strategy and correct the course regularly to progress on the path to success. Constantly reassess and revise your routines while keeping focused on your goals.

> "Always bear in mind that your own resolution to succeed is more important than any other."
>
> - Abraham Lincoln

Always be responsible for your actions and decisions, and maintain a relentless attitude to succeed. Again, learn from your mistakes and move on with your achievements. Always try to give a little more and go further than what is expected to advance in life.

Note that many people give up before achieving success, but victory is definitely for those who persist and maintain a positive and winning attitude. Celebrate your successes and reward yourself when you get good results, this will keep you inspired.

Daily personal triumphs can be something as simple as having successfully completed the "to do list" of tasks during the day or having been able to reach new customers or having managed to finish a report or taking the time to advance with your life project. Every day should be productive in one way or another. Even when you are at rest your mind can be focused on your goals for success. Constantly create and develop ideas and constructive thoughts and develop these with positive attitude always. Attend seminars with successful people and absorb all the knowledge they have to share and learn from those who have already traveled the road to success. This will strengthen your mind and give you more winning foundations for your personal development and progress.

Always visualize your goals and always keep a clear image of what you want to attain. Close your eyes and think that you already are in the place where you want to be in the way you want to be and review and analyze what steps you must follow to get closer to that goal. Always move forward, be persistent and even when you feel you have reached a goal, aim for a new one and stay active, as this will further strengthen your winning attitude and your positive mindset.

> *"Our greatest weakness lies in giving up. The most certain way to succeed is always to try just one more time."*
>
> – Thomas Edison

The Subconscious Mind and Positive Thinking

The Power of the Subconscious Mind

It is possible to have a positive thinking mind. Adoption of behaviors like daily positive affirmation and positive self-talk can change the brain's structure and ultimately influence the subconscious mind.

Then, how does the positive thinking work its magic in the mind? A combination of the subconscious and the conscious minds control life. Hence, altering their function may lead to new and different ways of being.

The subconscious mind is like an organic computer that produces certain results upon the insertion of information. It filters the "useless data" and focuses on the "important information." However, the definition of important and useless is mainly subjective. Below are examples of such scenarios:

Sound filters. After moving to a new house, one hears new sounds which did not exist in their previous homes. This happens since the subconscious mind is not acquainted with the sounds.

However, if listening is done keenly, sounds start to emerge such as a fridge working, a clock ticking, a dog barking in the distance, and a boiler switching on and off. Such familiar sounds are not heard since they add no value. Only unusual sounds are recognized, since they require attention.

Sight filters- One passes numerous cars which are not registered by the brain. But when one chooses a desirable car, it starts to appear frequently and even thinks that it's more common than others.

Perception filters on seeing, hearing, sensing etc. can have a major effect on decision making. For example, during a financial struggle, spotting a good deal might be hard since all the concentration is focused towards the lack of money.

Let's begin with definitions:

The Subconscious Mind

It is worth noting that the term subconscious mind does not exist in psychoanalysis since it's a new age self-development term that Freud called the unconscious mind.

The subconscious mind is the part of the brain that stores feelings, beliefs, desires, complexes and perceptions that are found outside the conscious awareness though they have powerful influence over the actions and behaviors at every moment.

The unconscious mind is associated with the reflecting, dreaming meditating and sleeping state. It's intuitive, and makes associations and connections between feelings, ideas and thoughts. It does the feeling and the perceiving.

The inner self talk

One has between 12,000 and 70,000 thoughts a day. A huge percentage of the thoughts are repetitive and about routine tasks that one undertakes each day. However, a small percentage of the thoughts come from one's internal self-talk. Does one have positive thoughts and use encouraging words which help them towards achieving goals or are they negative and destructive thoughts?

According to statistics, an average person has 70,000 thoughts each day of which a great percentage of them are negative. Worse still, some studies have suggested that negative thoughts are produced in much higher amounts and are comprises of 70% - 80% of the day's thoughts. Then it becomes crucial to administer these thoughts.

The conscious mind

It is the antithesis since it does all the intellectual thinking of the subconscious mind.

It is the mind responsible for self-talk, the endless stream of mind chatter that is capable of making someone crazy. It likes logical order and sequential information. It wants things to make sense and have reason. The conscious mind can handle awareness of 7-8 bits of information at the same time.

The magic of positive thinking and the subconscious mind

Most people think that they use their conscious mind to attract what they do in life, the *behavior,* but the truth is that the subconscious mind controls the larger part. Poor outcomes are the result of low expectations that are demonstrated when unconsciously an individual attracts the wrong things. Even if on a conscious level one makes the effort to achieve something, it will be difficult to achieve it unless one consciously has synergistic expectations.

Programming the subconscious mind

The conscious mind transfers information to the subconscious mind. Through the five senses, the conscious mind perceives the world. Then, judgment is attached to the thoughts, which creates feelings. The feelings are lodged into the unconscious mind as a belief.

Therefore, since all the unconscious thoughts were once conscious thoughts, one can program or influence the subconscious mind by adopting new thinking. That's how the magic of positive thinking applies. Through **daily positive affirmations** (http://positivemental-attitude.blogspot.com/) we are able to affect the subconscious mind.

Therefore, since all the unconscious thoughts were once conscious thoughts, one can program or influence the subconscious mind by adopting new thinking. That's how the magic of positive thinking applies.

The subconscious mind best understands the language of emotions. However, the positive and negative emotions cannot co-exist. Below are the major emotions.

The 7 major positive emotions:

· The emotion of FAITH

· The emotion of LOVE

· The emotion of SEX

· The emotion of DESIRE

· The emotion of HOPE

· The emotion of ROMANCE

· The emotion of ENTHUSIASM

The 7 major negative emotions:

- The emotion of ANGER

- The emotion of GREED

- The emotion of JELOUSY

- The emotion of HATRED

- The emotion of FEAR

- The emotion of SUPERSTITION

- The emotion of REVENGE

Impact your life by using the magic of positive thinking

Follow the 3 steps to help unleash the power of your mind by using the power of thoughts:

1. Be aware of negative programming and beliefs. Example, perhaps one was teased as many children are about their sports ability or a facial feature. And no matter what one does, it cannot come off our heads. One might have been "ugly" or "short" or "poor in sports." This is the negative thinking that needs reprogramming. You are what you think you are, not what others are trying to label you with. Keep in mind that as you see yourself others will perceive you. See yourself as a person capable of attaining what you want even if you fail. Convince yourself that if you try one more time you will most likely get there and even if you fail many times more, you now know that you learned a lot in the process.

2. Activate the thinking power-feed of the conscious mind with new beliefs. It is not important to agree with a new belief as long as it is motivating and one would like to believe it's true. In each case, "I am beautiful," "I am tall," "I am good at sports," or "I can do this" are the new beliefs that should be firmly instilled into your conscious mind.

3. Feed the conscious mind with continuous stimulus which aligns with these statements. Meditation-especially binaural brain beat meditation such as The Morry Method System and hypnosis are super vitamins. They help achieve a relaxed state of mind which makes it much easier to accept and integrate positive self-talk. Incorporate

daily affirmations and visualization exercises to make the change more rapid. The negative beliefs become much quieter as new positive stimulus are fed overtime. Start to listen to mind healing sounds that will help you focus on positive thoughts. Our minds are also governed by waves of energy that can be guided to move forward for positive outcomes. These positive vibrations and frequencies will make it easier for you to program both your conscious and subconscious minds while meditating.

Repeat these Positive Affirmations of Abundance:

- I am a prosperous human being, where ever I go I deserve abundance and prosperity
- The more grateful I am about life the more I receive
- I am capable of reaching all my goals and abundance flows through me

Repeated exposure to new beliefs and positive affirmations gives birth to new perception in the dedicated areas. At first, small changes are noticed like making a decision to take up a sport or learning new things. Learning something new is a great mind stimulant that always helps to build-up your self-confidence and your character. We, as humans, are natural born learners full of curiosity and when all this curiosity is canalized with consistent learning we achieve great results, making us more and more confident with our-selves. If there was a belief about being ugly, one may start to feel attractive and confident, which is translated by dressing smartly and taking care of our appearance to reflect the change.

Practice the magic of thoughts in life by controlling the thoughts you focus on. Positive thinking is among the best self-help solutions available and can do wonders for your life, remember you are in control!

Stop focusing on negative thoughts and embrace positive thinking now! A great idea always starts in the mind.

> *"We don't see things as they are, we see them as we are."*
>
> – Anais Nin

The Relationship Between Positive Thinking and the Law of Attraction

The law of attraction is the foundation of positive thinking. People can use this relationship to improve their lives, to become more successful and more productive. Many people have not realized that positive thoughts are the driving force behind the law of attraction. Every person wants to live a positive life where relationships are perfect, and success and money come easily. In a nutshell, the law of attraction states that we are what we think. Our lives are a result of our thoughts and beliefs. If you think negatively, your life will be negative. On the other hand, people with positive thoughts attract positive energy in their lives which helps them to be what they aspire to be. According to the law of attraction, the only way we can alter the direction of our lives is by changing our train of thought.

For the law of attraction to yield positive results, a person must have a positive attitude towards every aspect of life. According to the principles of the law of attraction, anger creates anger, fear engenders fear and failure begets failure. On the contrary, joy begets joy and peace begets peace. In short, a positive thought towards life will attract other similar positive outlooks. This has a magical snowballing effect. The logic behind these principles is that like attracts like. Human emotions and actions are contagious. That is why people laugh when they are in a crowd that is laughing and cry or share pain with those who are suffering, sick or in pain. Similarly, when a person is around successful people, she/he will tend to have positive thoughts about success, hence generating more success in his/her life.

There are some things that can obstruct the law of attraction. They include your attitude towards different aspects of life. For example, low self-worth and low confidence will continue to grow in you until they are altered through positive thoughts and self-love. Low self-esteem and low confidence are attitudes that form unconsciously in us. People with such attitudes will be inclined to focus their energy on harmful or negative things. The same applies to your body image. If you think and believe you are attractive, you will focus on maintaining your attractiveness by doing simple things like brushing your teeth, taking a shower, and combing your hair. Some attitudes are found in the unconscious level of thinking.

To achieve positive things in your life, you need to bear in mind that your thoughts and feelings are a form of energy that can generate both positive and negative influences.

Your thoughts and feelings attract people, things, incidents and deeds that have a similar influence as your thoughts and feelings. There are various ways you can use the relationship between the law of attraction and positive thinking to create a positive mindset. Once you adapt and apply these tactics, you will get positive outcomes in all your dreams and plans.

Tips to Enhance the Connection between the Law of Attraction and Positive Thinking

Lighten up- Always smile in every situation. Humor has positive therapeutic effects on physiology. Humor does not only lower stress levels, but it also helps people to shift perspectives. Because humor is a learned reaction, you should focus on developing and practicing a good sense of humor. For better results, humor should be accompanied by lots of laughter. Laughter is a physiological reaction to humor. Laughter relives stress, enables you to relax and have better sleep.

Do your best- For good results, do your best and have maximum focus on whatever you do. It makes sense to put a lot of effort in everything you do. Also ensure nothing distracts you until you have done well. When we do the best and focus on it, we bring out the best in other people.

Focus is a long term commitment that enhances consistency, thereby creating permanent positive thoughts in our minds. As a result, your dreams and plans become more realistic and the new positive energy will drive you to fulfill them.

Expect and hope for the best- After you have done your best, it is vital that you hope for the best. **If you believe you can make it, you will**. If you believe you cannot make it, you are very right! The positive or negative thoughts we have towards something can be a self-fulfilling prophecy. For instance, many firms run promotions and contests mainly for publicity. However, at the end of the contest, somebody must WIN. As a matter of fact, somebody ALWAYS wins. However, very few people enter the contests because they believe they cannot win. You should give your best and at the same time expect positive results. A positive mind will always attract positive results.

Listen to your instincts-Instincts are a product of an unconscious process, thus may be complex or tricky to describe or understand. Various people believe that instincts do not exist. However, they do exist. Just because bacteria could not be measured for a long duration of time did not mean they were non-existent. Many times your instincts are always right. Instincts always influence our decisions, such as doing something or going to some place.

Because instincts are based on incidences and situations in real life happenings, and experience is knowledge, most intuitions are right.

Use courteous words- Everybody in the society deserves respect. By using courteous words like "Thank you," "You're welcome,' "Excuse me," and "Sorry, we work to achieve a common good in the society. Courteous words make other people feel good and appreciated no matter their age, social status or gender. Just like a warm smile, courteous words create a human connection that is very valuable. Courteous words bring a smile to other people, thus attracting positive reactions from them.

The problem whether there is a relationship between positive thinking and the law of attraction has been debated several times until the present moment and, according to numerous psychologists, there is a very strong, clear and irrevocable connection between these two concepts.

The law of attraction is the common name for "like attracts like" and it is manifested based on people's mindset and way of thinking, not on their behavior or actions. This topic has been discussed a great deal during the last few years and, although there have been many documentaries, publications and seminars that have presented the connection between positive thinking and the law of attraction, people still do not have a very good understanding in this regard and their skepticism arouses suspicion to the majority of the world's population.

However, it is enough to analyze the theory attentively in order to draw a bottom line and find an appropriate answer for this concern. People's lives are often influenced by two major forces: one of them is their consciousness and the second one is what we call the "law of attraction." Consciousness is described as a person's quality to present awareness of external factors or other things that refer to them. Consciousness occurs only when people have the sense of selfhood and absolute control of their minds. Consciousness influences people's actions and lives. The principle is extremely simple: they are conscious; therefore they can react to different external factors.

Law of attraction is meant to help people achieve fulfillments of their dreams, wishes and expectations, but this concept is mainly influenced by their way of thinking. "Like attracts like" means "positive attracts positive" and "negative attracts negative." In other words, fear attracts fear, happiness attracts happiness, and laughter attracts laughter. It is highly unlikely to have a positive thinking attitude and attract a negative outcome; this would be practically a break of the law of attraction and the researchers concluded that it cannot happen based on their studies and experiments.

When you think positively, it means that you expect positive outcomes from your life – thus, you want something positive to happen, which can influence your life positively. When this happens, the law of attraction will allow you to reach your aim and, thus, something positive will really happen. If you want to move forward with your career and you have a positive perspective, the law of attraction will offer you exactly what you expect – no more and no less. But if you allow doubts and skepticism to influence your life, your thinking will slowly become negative, you will start telling yourself negative things and, in the end, the law of attraction will act accordingly; something negative will happen.

The principle of law of attraction is based on the positive or negative vibrations our thoughts and feelings create. When we think about something positive, we manage to attract people, situations, actions, circumstances and outcomes that create positive vibrations. On the other hand, thinking about something negative will create negative vibrations that will attract negative things, outcomes, people, etc…

Manifesting positive energy means attracting positive outcomes, so the law of attraction will offer you the opportunity to achieve all of your aims and fulfill your dreams.

Let's take a banal example: you are applying for a job and while you are waiting in the waiting room, you start doubting that you will be hired. In the end, the law of attraction will attract an inappropriate behavior, gestures, actions, words, thus resulting in a failure. If you think positive, the outcome will be positive.

Focusing on positive things will help you achieve them as a consequence of the law of attraction. You rarely or almost never can change a thing that is in the status quo, but you have the ability to change future situations and circumstances. If you face a financial breakdown and you keep thinking that you will never overcome it, the result will be either no change in your current problem (things stay in status quo) or a worsening, which will lead to losing money continuously and increasing your debts. It is important to focus on positive thinking, analyze your situation carefully and see what you can do to improve it –

in this way, the law of attraction will bring you a positive outcome, so you will manage to get out of debt.

Human feelings are considered contagious. When you laugh, other people will laugh; when you cry, other people will sense your sadness. Your thoughts are contagious for your life, as the law of attraction will react based on your optimism or skepticism. Practically, you will manage to create a chain reaction of positive situations and outcomes – if you think positively, you manage to find a solution for your financial problem; you solve it, so you continue to improve your financial situation. But remember the law of attraction works for those who take action; it is not enough to just want a lot of things, you need to act to make those things you want a reality.

The law of attraction has some powerful qualities as a placebo; this means that by focusing all your energies towards a positive outcome you then will gain control of a situation. Experiencing a placebo effect also means curing your diseases using the power of positive thinking, which is like having the healing effect when you get medication from a doctor. Many times a disease can be caused by a psychological disorder or weakness that also makes you weak and vulnerable. A strong positive mind makes you strong. The law of attraction is very similar – when you think positive, your problems tend to disappear and lose strength and your life will experience a major improvement. Analogically, you believe that you are taking adequate medication for your disease and you will be cured entirely (without actually taking the medication in question, though). It is all inside your mind and your beliefs affect the way your body feels.

The subconscious thinking is very important for the law of attraction; you might not be thinking something in a certain moment, but that something is somewhere in your subconscious, it exists. You have to adopt a positive thinking and eliminate doubts and skepticism completely and entirely if you want to experience a positive outcome of the law of attraction.

Drawing a bottom line, we can easily observe the strong connection between positive thinking and the law of attraction. According to Rhonda Byrne's self-help novel, "The Secret," "We become what we think about. Energy flows where attention goes" If we focus on positive things, we will create positive energy (vibrations), which will bring us a positive reaction from the law of attraction. As long as we adopt a positive thinking, we will attract positive outcomes.

For positive thoughts to manifest in our lives, we must consistently think positively. Positive thinking requires focus, commitment, hope and faith. It also requires us to wipe out negative thoughts and feelings which attract negative people, actions and circumstances. To achieve the most from the connection between the law of attraction and positive thinking, we must apply the law appropriately and wisely. It is very easy to do so as long as we are willing to transform our lives. A positive mindset will attract positive energy. Try it and the results will be amazing.

……....

There is unquestionably a very strong relationship between the "law of attraction" and positive thinking. This is mainly why a positive way of thinking is so effective and why it really works! This can be clarified as follows:

It is a fact that what you attract to your life is what you think…Period! You really are and you really become what you think. Your thoughts practically pave the way for the road to follow. The only way to change something in your life is to change the way you think. By programing your brain with systematic positive thoughts, those thoughts tend to become your reality.

So one must think there is a reason for this to happen, and the reason really is the law of attraction. Of course nothing happens by chance, with the law of attraction there has to be some action that is backed by a strong and solid positive thought. You just have to take a look at your own personal experiences. Examples of these recurring thoughts can be:

"I never have enough money to take care of my family or friends or me."

"I don´t like my job, I hate it! It makes me unhappy!"

"I am feeling sick all the time; I am tired!"

Negative thoughts like these ones will attract negative outcomes in your life. You are surrounding yourself with bad energy and attracting bad results. It sounds too basic but in reality this is how it is. If you hate something that something will most likely hate you as well! By hating your job, for example, you are putting an invisible shield between you and a better job opportunity that might come if you open your mind with a more positive attitude. With your negative thoughts you become blinded to other opportunities that may be all around you but you simply are unable to see them because your negative mind is blinding you!

There are always new opportunities, all the time, every day. But the secret is that you just need to be open to those new opportunities to start seeing them! Negativism makes you blind. It limits your thoughts and it limits you and your chance of a better outcome.

People that tend to trap themselves in negative thoughts limit their lives and their possibilities. It is like a self-inflicted imprisonment that keeps them away from good outcomes. It is all in their minds, remember you are what you think, and you attract what you think.

So what is the best way to change this?

If you think for a moment you will notice that there is almost an infinite amount of thoughts both positive and negative that constantly come into your mind. But do you really choose which thoughts will get into your mind at a certain point in time? In reality, this constant stream of thoughts comes in sort of a chaotic way where it is difficult to separate the good ones from the negative ones. This is where you have to train your mind to filter the ones you want to focus on. This requires a conscious action that recognizes which ones are negative and which ones are positive. The objective here is to consistently replace your negative thoughts by positive ones on a conscious level. The more you do this the more you will start to dominate what rules your mind and your way of thinking. You are in control, no one else!

You are the one who decides through your conscious filter which thoughts are the ones that are going to influence you. This is a very powerful technique that really works and when you learn to master this method it will become easier to be a positive thinker since your conscious mind will be affecting your unconscious mind. There has to be a systematic way of approaching your thoughts until you start seeing results. Now you are in control of your life and your decisions, and once you practice this more and more it becomes natural and you will be surprised with the changes this brings to your life, as it improves notably with this simple, yet powerful, technique. You are in charge. No one else is.

The magic of this way of approaching and managing your thoughts is that with more positive thinking, more positive results come your way. This is of course the law of attraction in full action. This is how you build your optimism. With good results your self-esteem starts to build up and this has a snowball effect that will ultimately affect your subconscious mind transforming you into a powerful positive thinker that is confident and knows that more positive thinking attracts even more good results, period! This has the magic effect of becoming a habit and a pattern that will flow naturally transforming your results in life in a positive way.

Once you start with this cycle of filtering your thoughts systematically you will start to attract positive outcomes into your life and you will become an optimistic by conviction. This is very powerful and it works!

Keep in mind that the more you focus on certain thoughts the greater the chances of those thoughts to become a reality. Of course, it takes time and concentration, but it will happen if you stick to your positive thoughts with faith and with action! Nothing happens without action. You are the one who is empowered to build your reality through your actions and your positive thoughts.

So start using the law of attraction and your positive thinking from now on! You are the one in charge, no one else is! The more you hold your positive thoughts in your mind the closer they will become your reality. These thoughts are vibrations of energy that will put into action the law of attraction by attracting good things on the same frequency. You will be given what you want and deserve, you just have to be persistent and remain positive no matter what! Remember you are in charge!

"There is little difference in people, but that little difference makes a big difference. The little difference is attitude. The big difference is whether it is positive or negative." – W. Clement Stone

Overcoming Negative Thoughts to Move Forward in Life

Overcoming past negative thoughts to move forward in life is not very complicated as long as you have ambition and you know that you want from your life. Every past event is a lesson for you, as it can help you improve yourself and avoid making the same mistakes again and again. Sometimes, certain events might seem unbearable and you simply consider it impossible to overcome them – however, what you really do not know is that there are many ways to deal with such unpleasant events, each of them offering you different possibilities and chances to go over your problems.

Positive thinking is surely a great way to overcome your past negative thoughts, because it will make you forget about your past mistakes entirely and learn how to never make them again. Several studies proved that having a positive thinking will increase the chances of receiving what you want or expect from your life, this principle is called the "law of attraction" like stated before, which is based on the "like attracts like" fortune. It is extremely simple, and you can easily approach positive thinking as long as you determine yourself to get over your past and start your life again. However if you think negatively, the outcomes will not be at all favorable for you or your future.

To overcome past negative thoughts, you will need to set yourself a goal, which you can achieve with your dedication and perseverance. Transform your positive thoughts into actions. Unless you forget about past failures and defeats in a constructive way, learning from them, they will always come to hunt you in your present life. You need to focus on something else, something you like, something you can dedicate all your resources, time and efforts to build your strengths each and every day – it maybe your career, your children or one of your hobbies.

But no matter what you choose, you need to understand the responsibilities you will have to take. It requires commitment and passion. Once you discover what you really like, your passion for it will awake naturally and even addictively in a positive way. Setting yourself a life goal will help you use your best qualities in order to do something positive and overcome your past negative thoughts in a way that is completely appropriate and safe for your mental health.

…..

Surprisingly, many psychologists recommend analyzing your past negative thoughts in order to overcome them and the principle they base their suggestion on is understanding. When you have a good understanding of yourself and every aspect that is somehow related to you, you are able to find proper solutions and learn how to solve your problems easily. Meditate about what mistakes you have made, study them closely and try to find a way to eliminate them forever from your life. Therefore, you will manage to transform negativism into positivism and failure into success – you will need to go through a dedicated process that will require all your mental resources, but you need to overcome your negative thoughts once and forever, so you can move forward in your life.

Love yourself. This is the best advice you can receive when it comes to negative past situations that target your life. Loving yourself, with all your qualities or faults, involves caring for your own good, which will analogically lead to a good understanding of your problems and a mature attitude that can help you solve them accurately. If you do not respect yourself, your self-esteem will start to fade away, leaving you in complete darkness and without any possibility of overcoming negative thoughts. You have to consider yourself a valuable person with many qualities – once you understand yourself, you will know how important it is to find a way to get rid of the negative thoughts. Take care of yourself and your health.

Relieving the stress you accumulated during the past might be a good way to eliminate the negative thoughts and rethink your life. In certain situations, stress will not allow you to do something good for you, because you will always feel somehow tense, without being able to think everything out clearly. Any activity you enjoy might be a good way to relieve stress and start thinking positive: sports, cooking, fishing, writing, going for a walk, listening to music, etc. Your brain needs to relax in order to eliminate the stress, so leave all your problems alone for a while and set aside a few moments for yourself every day. Nourish your spirit, and be confident with yourself.

Sometimes, your past negative thoughts might cause you a constant disturbance, and if that is your case, then it may be the right time to talk to a psychologist and share your most intimate thoughts or feelings with him so he can help you. But honestly, I think that you are capable of doing your own personal retrospective and evaluating your life and discovering all the good positive aspects that you have inside you. Then, you can turn them into your assets to move forward in life. Even though you made mistakes in the past and you encountered failure, you need to understand that everyone's life is based on the same principle, which oscillates between failure and success all the time. When you are ready to face your problems and find a good solution for overcoming them, your negativism will completely disappear and fade away.

Learning to forgive yourself is a good way to overcome your past negative thoughts, because feeling guilty will never allow you to move forward in your life. We have to be forgiving of ourselves and other people so we can let go and move forward. There is no such thing as a perfect human that never fails and it is important to understand this and stop blaming yourself while you learn from your mistakes. Your aim is to acquire as much knowledge from past failures and continue with determination no matter what happens and move on with the pursuit of your goals so you improve your life and gain confidence.

Once you understand that you are the only one who can control your thoughts, you will soon be able to overcome negative thinking and start seeing the positive side of everything around you. Everything related to the past is in the past and it cannot affect you anymore as long as you do not allow it to do so. Your future is waiting brightly for you to embrace it, so you need to leave alone negativism or anything related to your past and change the tone of your thoughts from pessimist to optimist.

"If someone tells you, 'You can't,' they really mean, 'I can't."

– Sean Stephenson

How to Set Goals to Achieve Everything You Want in Life

Everyone seeks success, but we all know that nothing comes easy. To achieve the success we spend a lot of time chasing, we first need to set goals. A **goal** is a fundamental component for attaining success in every endeavor, including in business. A goal serves as a guide to keep you on course when times get rough, and stop you from becoming distracted by insignificant matters. Regrettably, many people leave everything to chance. They believe they can't accomplish their goals, so fear hinders them from setting goals. Getting started may seem daunting, but I will show you how to seamlessly build up to it.

Know what you want

Before setting any goals, it's important that you know exactly what you want. Otherwise it's really difficult to get anywhere. If you are not clear with what you want, create a list of things that you want and things that you do not want. This will give you a good starting point. You may prefer to lose weight, attain a degree, buy a house, get a job, or set up a business. At this stage, don't think of how you are going to achieve the things you need so much, even if they appear impossible at first.

Know why you want it

One of the main reasons people fail to accomplish what they need in their life is that they don't know what is it that they want to achieve or don´t have any specific goals. You need to know why you want these specific things.

This is vitally important in goal setting, because if you don't have a strong reason for why you need this particular accomplishment for yourself, then you probably won't achieve it. Have a deadline too, as this will help you have a set time in mind in which you need to accomplish your goal.

Stay positive

You must be able to envision, taste, and comprehend the result you are chasing. All human achievements have been born out of visualization. Many top athletes routinely use imagination techniques to help them achieve success. By visualizing your objectives with close attention to detail, you're preparing yourself and ensuring you take the necessary steps to get there. Also, you can say affirmations time and time again to get you in the correct head space. You need to be as clear and thorough as you possibly can.

Set both long-term and short-term goals

Ideally, you have to set long-term goals and then smaller goals that are short-term and eventually tie in with the big picture. Many people set long-term goals and forget to set short term goals. Most long-term goals must have short term goals that lead to them. Not only does this make sense, but it also helps you stay focused. Short term goals are mini steps that help you accomplish your long-term goals faster. Both short term and long-term goals are important to one another.

Ensure that the goal is in your hand

You must be capable of achieving your goal thanks to your own determination, or with the willing help of the persons that are in your network. If you don't have control over the result, it doesn't make for a feasible goal. Keep in mind that unrealistic goals can ultimately lead to unforeseen amounts of stress. Do not put such fundamental things in the hands of what's the equivalent of slot machines; this would be like gambling with your future. There has to be a decided action in this process, or even a number of actions, the only way to accomplish the goals you have set is by taking action.

Set priorities

At any given time, you have numerous goals which are all in different phases of completion. Deciding which goal is more significant to you than others is imperative. For instance, if you have a work interview scheduled at the very same time as a training session with your personal trainer, then you should give priority to the one that represents more urgency in relation to your main goal.

Identify the challenges

Consider what kinds of barriers may stand in your way. After identifying the challenges, take the time to think of ways you can use to overcome them. There are internal and external barriers which will hinder you from achieving your goals. These are strong forces which will constrain you from accomplishing your goals.

External barriers are things we might not be able to change such as the weather, economical factors, family obligations, bottleneck traffic at freeway construction, the hours we work, budget, etc. Internal barriers are beliefs which drive our behavior. Emotional and psychological barriers are things like thinking you will always be overweight, I can't make it, I feel overwhelmed, it's too difficult for me to achieve this, etc.

Commit to your goals in writing

Imagine planning a trip without a particular destination in mind. What roads will you take? How will you even know when you've arrived? Instead, you begin by choosing the destination where you want to arrive. The same is true with the goals in your life. Writing down your targets forces you to pick a specific thing and decide what you need. The more successful you are, the more you will be flooded with new opportunities. Actually, these new opportunities can pull you off course. Writing your goals down will provide a filter for these opportunities.

Review you goals regularly

While settings goals has an upbeat effect on our accomplishments, there is one thing many people subconsciously tend to forget or overlook: reviewing their goals periodically. Reviewing your goals regularly is almost as fundamental as setting the goals in the first place. Our environment around us changes fast and it's our responsibility to adjust our goals so we can adapt to these changes. Review your goals regularly and provide honest feedback and try to adjust them as you go along. If you encounter blockades along the way, don't give up. Instead, modify them to meet your new requirements.

Among the best ways to build resilience and archive your goals is to define realistic objectives, although there is nothing wrong with dreaming big, in fact, your lifetime goal is your big dream where you have to focus all your energies. Setting goals may seem a little bit scary and too much responsibility, but it's easy to reach them if you take the right actions. With goal setting also comes responsibility and accountability and believe it or not this will keep you motivated and on track to your success.

"The difference in winning and losing is most often…not quitting." – Walt Disney

More on How to Set Goals

Most people feel that their lives are going nowhere and is without any direction, despite the fact that they work very hard. The lack of specific goal setting is what triggers this feeling of frustration. Your life is a serious journey that requires planning and you need a set of goals to follow so you know it has a purpose and a direction.

Setting goals is all about having a clear vision of where you want to be and what you want to achieve in life. It involves inspiration and the visualization of your future through a **positive thinking mindset**. Your goal is to turn your vision of your future into a tangible reality through step by step attainable phases that will become your objectives and ultimately are the steps you will climb to get where you want to be.

Goal setting is the most powerful tool you can use so you are able to measure your success on a daily basis. It shows you what your destination is before embarking onto your journey. When you have a goal you immediately know where to concentrate your efforts so you can reach that objective faster and easier. The process of setting objectives will help you find purpose in your life, as well as clarify where you want to be and what you want to accomplish.

Goal setting will keep you away from that frustrating feeling of not knowing what your life is all about. Goal setting equates to having a purpose in life, setting a north to follow, so you know when you are on track and closer to your objectives or when you have been derailed so you can make the required changes.

What is the purpose of setting objectives? It gives you motivation while you have a clear vision of where you want to go and what you want to accomplish. This is a very powerful tool that has been used by numerous successful individuals and athletes that have experienced the immense power of setting measurable goals to improve their performance and results and attain success. You don't know if you have accomplished something or reached a milestone unless you know you have crossed a preset line of purpose. If there is no goal then there is no objective to be reached, so you will not find the motivation to move forward.

Goals are set on different levels, personal levels, and lifetime objectives.

- You have to first visualize how you want to be in the long-term and set an attainable objective for the next five to ten years of your life. You have to ask

the question of how you see yourself a decade from now or five years from the present.
- After setting the big picture of your long-term objective in life you have to set small and clear to follow short term objectives.
- As soon as you have a roadmap you can start with your efforts to reach each one of the objectives you previously set always with a positive and optimistic attitude.

The reason for visualizing first the big picture is to make it easier to identify the steps that you need to take in order to accomplish your lifetime objective. By doing this you start to plan for the next five years of your life, for the next year, the next thirty days, for each day and once this objectives are defined you start working to attain them one by one.

The first step is to set your lifetime objectives:

Long-term goals are essential so you know in which direction you will be heading and it gives you a broad perspective of what is it that you want to achieve in the following years of your life. You can divide these objectives by categories:

- **Define Your Financial Goals**: how much money do you want earn this year? The following year? The next year? Five years from now? Set an attainable realistic target that you know you can accomplish and refine your targets and implement the changes you need to make to attain this number.

- **Define Your Career Objectives**: Your career or your work will help you attain your financial objectives in a determined amount of time. Think about what the steps are that you need to follow and the learning process you need to achieve in order to advance in your career or your work so you can get closer to your economic goals. For example, you may want to achieve a new position within your organization or your company. If so, you must think about the steps you need to follow to get into that new position and implement them.

- **Define Your Education Goals**: What new knowledge do you need to obtain in order to advance in your career or work? Are there any new courses, seminars, or knowledge that you need to learn in order to get a step closer to your objectives?

- **Define Your Health and Physical Objectives**: What are you currently doing to improve your health and take care of your body? Your health is a treasure that needs to be taken care of each and every day if you want to accomplish your life goals. A good physical condition is key to being able to advance towards your goals. A sick body will slow you down, but remember that by maintaining a positive attitude even your health will improve.

- **Define Your Family Goals**: Do you want to form a family? How large do you want your family to be?

- **Define How Do You Want to Spend Your Free Time**: Do you have a hobby or a sport that you want to practice while you are not working? How do you see yourself spending time on your health and with your loved ones?

- **Define Your Altruistic Goals**: How do you want to give back to society? What will you do once you achieve your dreams to help others achieve theirs? What type of legacy do you want to leave to your family and to the world?

All of these goals will help you define a life with a purpose, with a clear objective that will be more fulfilling to you and your loved ones. They will set the long-term picture. When you do this try to set some quiet time apart and be positive and ambitious and write down all of the ideas that come into your mind. Create a mind map that will help you to understand the steps you need to follow to achieve this dreams.

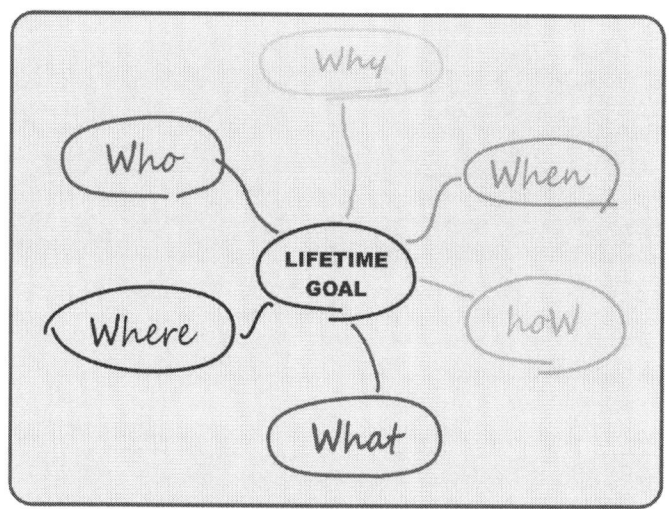

The second step is to identify your short term objectives:

Once you have a clear image of your long-term goals and how you see yourself in five to ten years, you need to break down these goals into smaller attainable pieces of objectives for a short term action plan.

Start with the steps you need to implement the next week, the next month and the following moths to get closer to where you want to be according to your lifetime plan.

Start by implementing a systematic To-Do Daily List that includes every step you need to follow aiming to the big picture of your lifetime goal. Your To-Do list will be defined by your objective, the clearer and more specific your objective is the easier it will be to come up with an attainable daily plan. Remember simple attainable and realistic objectives should be part of this daily roadmap so you can set the course towards your long-term objectives. Simple things such as collecting all of the available information and knowledge related to your lifetime goal are a great way to start. By setting goals your dreams will become a reality. Otherwise you will be living a day by day 9 to 5 life with no purpose.

How to Make Sure you are on Track to Achieving Your Goals:

Systematically review your To-Do list on a daily basis so you can make the necessary changes and identify new things that you need to add to your road map. Once you master this process it will come to you naturally. Use technology tools to plan your day like smartphone or tablet applications that will help you make notes and set daily goals. Always write down your goals as this will create commitment and accountability.

Your goals have to be:

- Attainable
- Measurable
- Specific
- Manageable
- Relevant

Once you define clear goals with an attainable and measurable set of time, you will know if you are on the right track and path to attain your long-term objectives. "I want to be rich" is a very vague goal; you have to be specific and set a short term attainable income objective first in order to advance to your next income target. For example you may want to earn more money next year or the following month, so you need to write down what the necessary steps are you need to follow in order to accomplish that income target, what set of new skills you need to acquire or what type of help you need to hire.

Always set dates, deadlines and even if you cannot reach those deadlines reset your plans and move on towards your goal. By setting measurable dates and times, you can evaluate your achievements and keep your motivation high.

Prioritize your goals so you don't feel overwhelmed and paralyzed by the amount of work you have ahead of you. Go step by step with a clear direction in mind and give more weight and attention to your main objectives by keeping the big picture always present.

Leverage is a very important tool you want to implement in your life-plan if you want to accomplish more in a shorter period of time. Remember to reward yourself every time you achieve one of your goals and celebrate each victory so you nourish your self-esteem and your motivation. And remember you must always have a "YES I CAN DO THIS" attitude to succeed! BE POSITIVE!

"You are never too old to set another goal or dream a new dream." – C.S. Lewis

How to Attract Abundance through Positive Thinking

If you want abundance, you have to practice positive thinking and have a positive mindset. Whether you want a lot of money, a ton of happiness, or an endless supply of healthy relationships, you have to be in the right attitude in order to have those things. If you don't feel as though you deserve it or have the ability to get it, then you are not going to allow people and situations into your life that help you achieve it. This is simply the law of attraction.

If you are not convinced about the law of attraction, then you should know that research is proving the fact that positive thinking helps draw abundance into your life. The only way to attract abundance is to step outside of your comfort zone and bring new things into your life. Evidence suggests that positive emotions, caused from positive thinking, help to improve attention, cognition and action, which helps to build social, physical and intellectual resources.
[Source:http://www.ncbi.nlm.nih.gov/pmc/articles/PMC1693418/pdf/15347528.pdf].

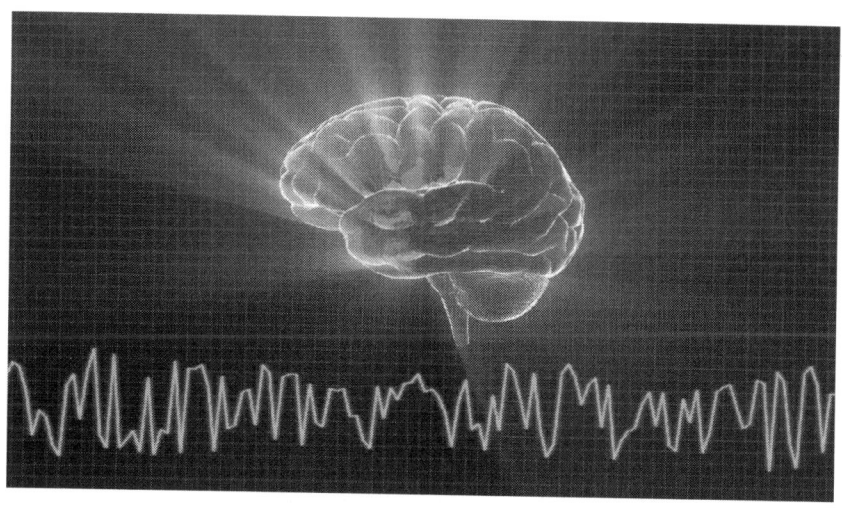

In addition, since action is needed to attract abundance, energy is also needed. Negative thinking is quick to drain energy from the body and leave you feeling as though you don't want to do anything. This is something that we have all experienced. When negative thinking becomes overwhelming, it is much easier to curl up on a couch than it is to get out and take action on the things we want.

How to Start Incorporating Positive Thinking into your Life

Positive thinking does not happen overnight. Just as it takes years to develop a negative mindset, it can take a while to develop a positive mindset. It takes practice and commitment to think positively. The benefits of it, including attracting abundance into your life, is well worth the practice. The following are some proven ways to shift your mindset to a permanently positive state.

1. Always Look on the Positive Side of Things

It is very easy to see the negative in any situation. For instance, if someone cuts you off in traffic, it is easy to focus on what a jerk that guy is and how he affected your day in a negative way. To develop a positive mindset, you have to be able to look at a situation and pull out the positive aspect of it. The main problem is that the positive aspects may not always be completely visible. For instance, someone cutting you off in traffic may result in you avoiding an accident up ahead. The more you look for the positive aspect of the situation, the easier it will become to find it.

While this is useful in getting over negative experiences, it can also help you find value in experiences and encourage you to take action towards abundance. For instance, if you try to start a business and you fail, looking at the failure as a lesson that will help you avoid similar mistakes in the future. It will ensure that you move forward with a higher chance of success than ever before. In other words, every time you fail and view it as a positive lesson on what 'not' to do, you move closer and closer towards your goal.

Eventually, you will reach your goal and have what you want. It is only a matter of time, but rest assured that through a positive attitude and mindset, every dream is attainable. Again, the law of attraction will be on your side, if you just give it a chance!

2. **Be Grateful**

There is a reason the gratitude is talked about by every single successful person in the world: it is very powerful. Being grateful helps you to see positive things that occur in your day. People who do not practice gratitude have a hard time pulling positive aspects out of their own lives and, instead, focus on the negative. The more you consciously practice being grateful, the more you will consciously look for things to be grateful for, and when you do that it becomes very hard not to practice positive thinking. This is a very powerful aspect that only requires from you a grateful attitude towards the good things in life. We sometimes take too many of the simple things we enjoy every day for granted. We don't realize that these little things are privileges that other people don´t even enjoy. Being grateful not only attracts abundance to your life, but it also makes you enjoy more the simple things that keep you alive and well each and every day.

Commit to practicing gratitude. When you wake up in the morning, write down what you are grateful for before your mind has a chance to focus on anything else. You may want to write about the great night's sleep you had, or the things you're looking forward to throughout your day or just simple things such as your pillow, your bed, and the hot water in your shower. Starting your day off with a positive mindset will help you to continue to have a positive mindset throughout the day and work towards your goals and desires. This is simple, yet very effective.

3. **Take Responsibility for Your Life**

Maintaining a victim-like mentality will never help you consistently practice positive thinking. Instead you will blame others for why you have not received the things you want and that will hold you back from taking action and going after what you want. When you don't take responsibility for your own life, you are actively participating in negative thinking at every turn.

"He did this to me!" and "She is the reason I cannot take the next step towards my goals!" These are the kinds of statements that lead you towards more negative thoughts and push abundance way.

Take responsibility for everything that happens in your life. When you do, you will stop making excuses for why you don't have what you want, and you will start creating a life that you do want and deserve. Remember, you choose your behavior, responses and thoughts. No one else can help you attract abundance into your life, just as no one else can keep abundance away from you. You deserve abundance. You just have to focus on attaining your goals by keeping a forward thinking positive attitude and by accepting responsibility. No one else is responsible for your future, you are the only one!

4. Remove Negative People from your Life

The people you surround yourself with have a huge influence over how you think. For example, it is very easy to get caught up in a negative conversation with someone who always focuses on the negative, and this can shift the way you view situations or people.

Even if you do not think that negative people are influencing your life in a negative way, you'll be surprised to learn that their words, actions, and even their energy, affects your life in some way. They likely produce some level of stress on your body and mind [Source: http://www.psychologicalscience.org/index.php/news/releases/research-explores-how-our-relationships-can-impact-our-health.html], and stress is not a friend of positive thinking.

This is something that has to be experienced to understand. Once you remove negative people from your life, it is easy to see how much lighter and more positive you feel.

You may not always be able to remove negative people from your life completely, but you can limit the amount of interaction you have with them. While it may seem like an impolite thing to do, the truth is that your happiness and abundance depends on it, and you get the final say over your life.

In the end, positive thinking helps you attract abundance by encouraging you to accept circumstances and people into your life that help you achieve the things you want. In addition, it gives you the energy you need to keep moving forward towards your dreams and desires. Once you consistently start to practice positive thinking, you will notice more and more positive experiences and people moving into your life, and you will begin to attract everything you have wanted with ease.

"Success consists of going from failure to failure without loss of enthusiasm."

– Winston Churchill

How to Improve Your Self-Esteem and Become a Positive Thinker

Self-esteem has a direct correlation with the potential happiness and success a person can have in their life. When a person is struggling to be happy with him-self, it is virtually impossible for this individual to provide and project happiness to others. With self-esteem, there is a wide array of factors that will affect how a person thinks about his own condition. At the root of its meaning, self-esteem is how a person deals with their faults. If a person believes that he is not adequate to perform a job or different duties, that no one will like them or that they are simply not good enough, it will be impossible for them to become a positive thinker.

Unfortunately, a person that suffers with this problem will find that others do not want to be associated with them. Why is this? Negativity can be a plague, wherein others will start to become depressed or have negative thoughts about themselves too. Negativity and positive thinking can be contagious. It all depends on which side you decide to be on. This, however, can be turned around by promoting a way of thinking that nurtures self-esteem and positivity.

Positive Thinking Breeds Positivity

Positive thinking allows a person to finally break free from the psychological constraints that they put on themselves. Instead of waking up every morning dreading the work day, think of all of the things that you are going to be able to accomplish that day. Even if it is just one thing, focus your mind on completing that specific objective on a particular day. Again, the sense of accomplishment is a great self-esteem builder that leads to a more positive way of appreciating life. By being a positive thinker, something magical happens – the law of attraction starts to actually work in your favor.

The Law of Attraction is a direct result of the positive and negative thoughts that a person has during their life. When negativity surrounds a person, bad things are sure to follow. However, when a person has all of the luck in the world, there is usually a reason. These are positive individuals that are able to overlook and learn from their faults, as well as the faults of others. Weaknesses are turned into strengths by analyzing their causes and learning from them. Through this positive thinking, they are able to achieve the one thing a negative person is never able to – receive positivity in return. With this one change, a person will be able to boost their self-esteem. However, there are many proactive ways to increase self-esteem and start thinking positively in the process. Expose yourself to positive thinking images every morning and think about their meaning in a constructive way. Be inspired by these images and embrace their encouraging message. Use your intelligence to generate ideas and analyze them while you brainstorm for new solutions when you pursue your goals. This will keep you encouraged and with a sharp mind thinking positively.

Tips to Boost Positivity and Self-Esteem

Self-esteem and positive thoughts are able to be changed drastically with minimal effort. The following tips will ensure that a person gets out of their slump and back on track to a happy and constructive outlook in life:

Eliminating negative friends: There are always friends in a person's life that never seem to be happy. When a minor life problem occurs, they will view it as the end of the world. While it is always admirable to be a good friend, these are the types of people holding others back from true happiness. If a friend is always negative, removing this person from your social circle can yield a whole new outlook on life.

Find positivity: Life is always going to show a person happy and difficult circumstances. Instead of letting the negative factors always hold prominence over the positive factors, you should change this mindset. Losing a job is horrible, but finding a new job may result in a better economic compensation in a better professional situation and provide a superior learning experience. Every situation has positive aspects and thinking on the bright side will produce a higher self-esteem and increased positivity.

Meditation: Meditation has great benefits. One of them is building positivity and mind control. Through meditation, a person is able to put aside all of the stresses of the day and start to focus on the positive aspects. This leads to increased happiness and a better understanding of what needs to be done to turn a negative situation into a positive one.

Fitness and Health: Through yoga, sports, or regular exercise, you will be doing something positive for your body and your self-image. A person that is physically fit and takes care of their body by eating healthy foods will ensure that their health never gets in the way of true happiness. A fit, energetic person is ready to take on the world every day. Your health is a treasure, so always try to be healthy and take care of your body. By treating your body well you are treating yourself well and building self-esteem at the same time. Detox your body and be healthy! When you feel healthy you feel strong and capable to undertake and face any challenge in life.

Help others: Inner happiness and positivity can be found through many different avenues. However, helping others can often change a person's entire perspective on life. The problems every person has will be different. Helping people to overcome their problems may lead to the understanding that your own circumstances are not as bad and that things could be worse. In fact, knowing that another has been helped can create a world of positivity in itself. Always be grateful for what you have and for what is working for you right now and try to build on those strengths to advance in life. Volunteering also builds your self-esteem by having a proud sense of achievement knowing that you helped others in need. This has a power of reciprocity that ultimately will affect your life in a constructive and positive way. Do good and you will receive good in exchange.

Analyze: The most successful people in life are those that want to understand their faults and improve upon them. Through analyzing oneself, as well as a situation, it will be possible to grow your self-esteem and start to find positivity. Perhaps there were far more positive attributes to a situation than you originally thought.

Start the day positively: Waking up in the morning and starting the day with a positive outlook can impact a person's life dramatically. A good way to achieve this positive frame of mind is to read an inspirational quote in the morning. Through this routine, a person will have a higher sense of value and ensure that their day is positive from the start.

Moving Past the Negative Thoughts and Situations

The more positive thoughts a person has, the higher their self-esteem will be. There will always be times when a person fails, is rejected or simply is not happy with themselves. However, this is something that happens to every person during their lifetime. Instead of dwelling on these moments, learn to move past them and even embrace the negative aspects at times as tools that will be necessary and helpful to confront new problems you might face in the future.

Every person is able to describe their faults and weaknesses; negative thinkers give a low weight to their positive attributes instead of emphasizing the bright aspects he or she has. Positive thinkers, however, will find that their faults are truly great aspects of their success. While a person may be a terrible procrastinator, this may also have taught them that adhering to a strict schedule that allows them to be more productive.

Being happy with yourself and having high self-esteem is not an overnight process. The more good energy a person is able to produce, the faster they will see results. Through positivity, it is possible to stop dwelling on all of the weaknesses, and start realizing that every person and situation has good aspects as well. You can decide to focus your mind on positive things or on negative ones. It takes just about the same amount of effort from your brain to close your eyes and envision a wonderful day as it takes to picture yourself in a bad situation. You decide! You are not a prisoner of your thoughts; you can control them and decide which ones will make you grow!

"The will to win, the desire to succeed, the urge to reach your full potential... these are the keys that will unlock the door to personal excellence."

– Confucius

A Guide on How to Eliminate Negative Thinking, Stress and Fear

If you ask, many people will tell you that stress is stress and it is normal to be stressed, but this is wrong. Stress is not normal and it's something that we should all strive to eliminate in our life. It's a product of negative thinking or fears that we face. Stress can stream from thoughts of events that happened in the past, events that are taking place presently in your life or uncertainties associated with future events. For example, stress can result when you think about a fight that broke up between your loved one (past event), concerns about whether what you are doing is right (present events) or fear of whether your shares will perform well in the stock market (future events).

When most people think about what stresses them out, what come in their mind are things like relationships, money, health concerns or their never ending to-do list. To them, removing stress means coming up with new things to do. They look at situations in their life that they can change, things they can do differently, or responsibilities they can do away with to create a "balance" in their life. But do they manage to get rid of stress in their life?

The answer is *no they don't*. First, if you are to remove stress in your life, you have to tackle its main cause: your thoughts and fears. Yes! Whenever, you allow yourself to dwell in fearful and negative thoughts, you create stress.

If you really want to get rid of stress in your life, it's time to move from fearful and negative thinking. It's the only way that will leave you feeling renewed and recharged in all aspects of your life. I mean, you will have to get away from treating artificial causes of stress and work on the main cause. Well, you may not have control of what is happening in your life, but you do have control over how and what you think about it. You just need to unplug from the three main causes of fear and negative thinking namely:

· Negative self-talk about yourself

· Negative self-talk about situations

· Negative future fantasizing-fear

Well, I know now you are wondering how I am just expecting you to think positively about awful things that are happening in your life…let's say you just lost your job. The truth is that if you choose to focus on the positive side of it, you will have less stress and you will be able to move on. Always seek to find out what you have gained from each of your losses as opposed to dwelling on counting how unfortunate you have been. It's one great way to effectively kill negative thinking. For positive thinkers every loss is an experience learned so you know how to be better next time. It is about a change of attitude towards things and why they happen.

To effectively fight fear in your life, you will have to appreciate that as a human being, you exist in the present. The present moment you are in is the only thing that is real. Your past does not exist today and it's therefore no longer real. The future which has not yet occurred is also not real. Only your life today and what happens at this moment is real and that is where you should live. It's what your mind should concentrate on. Move away from future worries. All you can do about the future is to plan adequately for it.

Well, I know you are stressed. Of course, at some point we all are, and we all have to pay the bills at the end of the month and probably a huge mortgage balance. What I mean is that you are not stressed because of actual problems. You are stressed because you are afraid you may not be able to pay your bills or come up with the money needed to support your family or yourself or your current health condition. You don't think you can pay the bills and you don't think your job is going to get any better. The truth is, if you adopt a positive thinking mindset, all these worries and the related stress would all be a thing of the past. Look at things with optimism. Yes, even your own health can be affected by the perception you have about it. If you think you are able to heal than your body will certainly react accordingly by feeling better. Sometimes stress is a feeling of self-inflicted anguish that can be solved by achieving clarity of mind and by facing each problem one by one. Every little step we take towards addressing the causes of our stress is a win in positive thinking.

To get a step higher in eliminating stress and negative thinking in your life, focus on what you have and appreciate it. If you are fortunate enough to have a job…appreciate it, and think of ways to get a new one if you don't like your current position. Always think constructively not destructively; always be proactive and not inactive and passive. If you have a family-enjoy every minute of the company they give, be always grateful for their love. Of course you can feed them today-that is enough for this present moment; if you would like to buy them a house, that will be in the future and it should not worry you. Get your mind to think this way and you will even have time to plan your future and overcome the negative thinking that have been torturing your mind and stressing you.

Another great tip that will save you from stress arising from negative thinking and fear is to realize that fear and negative thinking is just "fear and negative thinking." They are nothing more than that. Negatives, fear and stress take you over the moment you start giving them attention. So, stop giving them attention. Always focus on the good thoughts, not on the negative ones.

It's true. If you keep yourself having fun in an environment that is free from loneliness, you will not end up thinking negatively. Involve yourself in something that gives you fun like watching a movie or taking a night out with a friend or your loved one or just going for a walk and being in contact with nature in a park. Sometimes, all that your mind needs is to "talk" things out or to see someone around. Human beings are meant to be social. Do not isolate yourself or otherwise you will dwell in the world of fear and negative thinking. This is the principle applied in solitary confinement of criminals. You are not a criminal, so don't torture your mind with loneliness. Read about what you like, and always build your positive mind, as reading inspirational books will relieve your stress and motivate you.

In addition, you need to spend some time doing things that can recharge your mind with uplifting thoughts even without having people around. The top two of these activities are:

Take some time and think about gratitude. Writing in a journal about things that you appreciate and love can be a good therapy or a good road map to plan ahead. When you put things in writing you commit to those things, so in order to advance and be more proactive, write down a "to do" list every day. This will keep you away from negative thoughts and give you the sense of accomplishment that will help you build up your confidence and your positive thinking mindset.

Think about an inspired vision that you hold in your mind about your own future and write it down. This will help you visualize what you are trying to accomplish. Embark on new projects even if they seem to be little ones, as this will help you maintain a focused positive attitude.

Eliminating fear, stress, and negative thinking in your life does not mean you bury your head in the sand and ignore the pressures in your life. It means you approach unpleasant situations in your life with positivism. Always think and expect that the best is going to happen and not the worst. This is the key to eliminating fear, negative thinking and stress in your life.

All of your most fundamental worries are basically caused by just mind blocking illusions that ultimately become the governing pattern of your behavior. Negative affirmations like the following:

- I am unable to enjoy life because I hate the job I have.
- I just can't lose weight because it is too difficult.
- I just work to pay my bills.
- I am no longer pursuing my dreams; I just don't have the time, etc.

All these negative affirmations become frustrations and they block you, replace all these negative thoughts with powerful positive affirmations. You have to improve your self-esteem to overcome all these negative frustrations and become a positive thinker. One way to improve your self-esteem is by taking action and work relentlessly towards your life objectives. A low self-esteem can be the root of all of these frustrations. Start believing from now that you deserve good things. Once you change how you see yourself and attain full confidence, you will be able to achieve everything you want in life.

Discover the 10 Laws to Unleash the Power of Positive Thinking

Discover the magic of positive thinking and the ten rules that will help you to achieve a progressive momentum effect. Today most people recognize that there is truly a hidden magic in positive thinking. What better than a set of simple rules to approach this way of thinking and to help you move forward with your life. It all depends from the perspective you look at things, while some people may see an empty glass with the prospect of filling it others may see it as a sign of failure and that all is finished for them.

We as human beings have control of our thoughts and our destiny if we have a positive approach to what we do and how we see things. Failure is just a battle lost and a lesson learned for those who are determined to believe in themselves and determined to move forward. In fact, the world's most successful people have accumulated several defeats from which they have learned and come out stronger because they believed in the magic of positive thinking.

An idle brain is a crop of demons that destroy a person's purposes and will. Keeping your brain active and a sharp mind should be the first step towards a more positive and creative personality. Productivity and creativity are born from an active mind that is constantly exercising its thoughts. We can achieve positive results when our minds are fully functional and this ideology should be the basis of a winning attitude for a more productive you. The idle mind is a lazy mind that is vulnerably affected by negative thoughts. The ideal way to combat this problem is to concentrate our thoughts in a creative process that allows us to develop these rules and advance in the right direction, towards an unlimited prosperity.

> *"If you think you can do a thing or think you can't do a thing, you're right."* – Henry Ford

Below are the 10 main rules to develop the magic of positive thinking:

1) Believe - We have to believe! You cannot pretend to be a positive thinker if you don't believe in your own self, there is got to be a deep conviction that you are capable of achieving something. Positive thinking cannot be feigned because there is nothing to pretend, it's just a matter of believing. You project what you believe and this is probably the most important rule of all and you owe it yourself to

believe. You are in control of your mind, no one else is; only you can decide whether to believe or not believe something is possible. Whether your past experience has told you something is not possible, what matters is the conviction of knowing that if you believe it is possible and try it again and again, then the magic will happen! Cultivating this quality is essential to advance towards the magic of positive thinking.

There is a tendency to give up and to doubt about our abilities, but there is another even more powerful trend in people who want to succeed and that is the persistence and the self-belief that you can achieve what you want, to tirelessly believe that something is possible. We have to detoxify our minds from negative thoughts that keep us from attaining what we really are capable of. We have to get rid of our own psychological barriers that are just a self-imposed type of disease that keeps us trapped in a negative world. So start BELIEVING RIGHT NOW THAT YES, YOU CAN DO IT AND YOU WILL!

2) Always have a goal, an objective - This aspect is one of the most important within the 10 rules to unleash the magic of positive thinking. Many people tend to evaluate their lives for their failures and thus lose all hope of

achieving their goals. When you don't have a goal it is very difficult or almost impossible to achieve something. How on earth are you going to know where you want to get if you don't set a destiny, a purpose, an objective. Having a goal is a fundamental element that builds and nurtures your positive mind. Start by having short-term goals to achieve larger long-term objectives. The first step to reach the end of the stair climb is always the first step. If you fall while starting your climb the first time, you just have to try it again, it is human and natural to fail, what really matters is that you are able to visualize the steps and be focused on your target so you can keep on trying no matter what. The objective must be clear and measurable so we know when we have attained it. Short term goals are great to achieve this purpose. They can be simple, but measurable goals, such as having the objective of accomplishing something realistic each day.

This rule of having something achievable and measurable every day gives us a very important element that feeds the positive mind and our motivation. When we are motivated our positive mind is stimulated to move forward and the self-belief that something can be done is reaffirmed so we head towards the next step with more confidence. Successful people who reach their targets are the people who set objectives as a way of moving forward. Once a goal is reached, they continue and endure setting new goals. Having a goal should not be the final destination, but a continuous way of thinking where objectives are constantly renewed to further stimulate the magic of positive thinking.

3) Surround yourself with people who have a positive attitude. When you are involved in an internal battle between the negative and positive, you will need all the help and support they can give you. Never surround yourself with negative people that become a burden that infects you with weakening thoughts of defeat. Conversely, when you are surrounded by people with positive thinking, you combine energies that result in a power that will propel your life to move forward and these type of people are the support you need in moments of faintness and mental weakness.

But is not enough to surround yourself with positive thinking people, consume all the possible content material you can find such as books, empowering videos, and seminars that will make it easier for you to move towards a more positive attitude. I mean books like the one you are reading right now that emphasize the powers of positive thinking to radically transform your life and achieve everything you want. Our mind is programmable. It all depends on what instructions you want to give to your brain. Hence the importance of goals, these are the basis of the instructions of role models or guides to achieve what you set out to accomplish.

4) Have a Healthy Life. No matter how positive you are, it would not be of any help if you are dead! It should be a priority to maintain a healthy and detoxified body if you want to feed your positive thinking attitude. Watch your diet, exercise your body as much as possible. Walk whenever you can and enjoy a relaxing walk in the park or a bike ride to dissipate and refresh your mind. This will help you relax your brain and charge it with positive thoughts. Get in touch with nature as often as you can and always be thankful for your good health, for your life and for having a lucid mind.

A key step to attain the magic of positive thinking is by taking care of your body and your mental health. With a sick body and an intoxicated system and a sick mind it is virtually impossible to achieve your proposed goals and this is a physical burden that keeps you away from your objectives. Clean your body and maintain a healthy and clear mind. Drink lots of water, clean water keeps your body fresh and hydrated and also gives you mental clarity. There is no other liquid on earth more transparent and refreshing than water and it is a very powerful element of nature that goes hand-in-hand with the power of positive thinking. Build and feed your inner body and soul to project your best image on the outside. When you feel great inside you create good energy.

5) Change the negativity around. Remove all negative thoughts and actively repel everything negative that comes into your mind. Direct that energy into positive thoughts. Positive affirmations will help keep negativity away and far from your thoughts and your mind.

6) Be patient. Positive thinking is not attained immediately. You need to be reprogrammed so you are able to eliminate any negative attitudes you have. This is part of a process that begins with achievable goals and it is reinforced each time you accomplish one of these. Patience is a virtue that we must learn to cultivate since immediate gratification and instant success does not happen very often in real life. Instead what really happens if you are persistent is a series of small continued successes when measurable and realistic goals are set. We must have the patience and the persistence for these successes to happen so we continue to build the magic of positive thinking.

7) Remember that people can feel your negativity. Improve your attitude. Before undertaking anything in your life, make sure you have the right attitude. One of the reasons people fail is because others may perceive their negative attitude and do not want to do anything with this. Adopt a positive thinking attitude and a way of seeing things in a constructive way. This also creates receptiveness to

receive positive affirmations and feed your optimistic attitude.

8) Maintain an Unbreakable Positive Attitude. Always find something positive in all aspects of life. When you encounter something unfamiliar or unexpected, do not be afraid. Always look at things from an optimistic point of view and see the good aspects that these entail, this will make your life easier and bearable, thus building your positive mind.

9) Keep pace and prevail. You need to pace yourself to prevent collapsing. Take life one day at a time and do not despair. Remember that you cannot hurry and expect immediate results, good things and outcomes should not be forced, they will come naturally as you prevail and persist. Be patient, but keep the pace. In this way you will achieve a positive attitude. Keeping pace means to move forward always with a purpose, do not lose your north; stimulate your mind with your goals in order to keep your motivation in a natural and spontaneous way.

Every day, when you wake up in the morning, always think about what you can do today to get a step closer to your goals so you can keep up moving forward. Set the steps one day at a time. A great way to accomplish this is to write down your list of tasks to complete during the day every day. By planning your day, you will know which tasks you successfully completed during the day and which ones you missed so you are able to keep pace and move toward your goals so you discover the magic of positive thinking.

10) Apply the rules for positive change. The main feature of these 10 rules of the magic of positive thinking is the fact that you will get closer to the door that connects your goals with your achievements. You must open this door. Many people do not realize this, but we need some standards and rules in order to make it easier to track our success. Some people think rules limit our achievements, but this is false. Without any rules, we would not have achieved a purpose or reached any goals as human beings. Directions help us to eliminate the chaos and disorganization by imposing a path to follow. This makes it easier to move forward with our lives and it is easier to achieve a positive lifestyle and measurable and visible positive results. These guidelines are intended to be elements of support and guidance to achieve your goals. They are also used to give a purpose to your life. A life without purpose is a life that is adrift, and lacks encouragement to keep going, and the lack of inspiration gives room for negative thoughts.

Apply these 10 simple rules, and discover the magic of positive thinking now!

"If you can dream it, then you can achieve it. You will get all you want in life if you help enough other people get what they want."

– Zig Ziglar

How to Relieve Stress to Advance with Your Life Goals

Prioritizing and realistic goal setting is a way to reduce stress, so you can accomplish more in life without torturing your mind. You can feel overwhelmed when you have a seemingly endless "To-Do list" that seems almost impossible to accomplish. The best way to reduce stress is by going on a step-by-step agenda, giving priority to the tasks that are more important and relevant in relation to your main goals.

To relieve stress, you must decide the order in which you want to start working on every task you have planned every day. You have to first define very clearly what is it that you want to pursue so you can plan accordingly. Prioritizing is giving more importance to the tasks that need immediate attention so you can continue with the less vital things on your list. Once you decide what you want, things will begin to appear more clearly. The following is a plan you can use to reduce your stress levels and feel less overwhelmed:

- **Define Your Main Goal First According to What You Really Want**. This is a crucial aspect of your prioritization and it is the root of your macro plan. You have to be as specific as you can be and define exactly what is it that you want to pursue and accomplish and set a realistic time frame to get there. Close your eyes and think positively and profoundly about your dream and write it down in a place where you know you will be able to access it when you need it. It can be a journal, an application or in a digital format document, but make sure you write it down.

Remember, this creates commitment and it will be the base of your planning. Think about all of the reasons you have to pursue this dream and also write them down. Why are you following this goal? You have to have a strong purpose that moves you forward and motivates you. Writing down this lifetime goal will reassure you when you feel you want to just give up and when you feel weak. Whenever this happens go back and reread your main goal and the reasons you have to pursue this main objective so you can keep your motivation high in times of faintness.

- **Start Planning and Write down a Plan to Achieve Your Main Goal.** Set short term goals in order to get closer to your main objective. Write these small objectives down in a daily planner and save them. This will be your roadmap in case you get derailed for some reason. Never be discouraged and stick to your master plan so you move forward and eliminate stress with every little task you accomplish. A task manager app can be very helpful if you want to make sure you accomplish each and every one of your tasks. Learn to delegate to reduce stress and use leverage to accomplish more in less time. Once you get into a position where you can hire assistance to help you complete your daily tasks it will be easier for you to manage your time and accomplish more so you get closer to your main goal in less time. In today's age and era we have technology on our sides and a myriad of online applications and websites where you can hire help for a relatively low cost. You can have a virtual assistant to help you with repetitive tasks that are time consuming so you can focus on the big picture and relieve stress. This way you will also increase your productivity and accomplish more. Always be organized.

- **Commit to Your Plan and Do It**! No planning and no goal setting will ever work if you don't take action. Action is a must if you want to ever see results. Paralysis by analysis is not an option and you have to be actively working on your plan and completing daily tasks so you beat procrastination. Don't spend hours or days contemplating and analyzing your plan, just do it! Take action now so you can start seeing results. This is the only way in which you will get closer and closer to your goals, by taking action; so stop dreaming and make those dreams a reality now! Stick to your positive mindset and you will see the results you want faster than you ever thought possible! In order to run we must first walk and the first steps are always the most difficult.

You know you can do it, so don't let any stress or any fear of failure destroy your dreams and advance with your life plan now!

Once you start on your path to success, you will know better how to manage stress or any temporary defeat because you know you already have a master plan you can follow. You know what your destination is, and the name of that destination is achieving your goals. No goal will be ever be attained if you give up. Always enjoy your journey because there is a lot of learning through that journey and a lot of experience is acquired while you move forward with your lifetime plan. Success will come your way once you manage your stress and prioritize by always sticking tirelessly to your main objective. Remember to be realistic by remaining positive at the same time. We are not robots, but we surely can accomplish a lot of things if we decide to pursue them.

Positive Thinking and Success - Changing Your Life through the Magic of Positive Thinking

You have to be honest with yourself and recognize that you are where you are today because of yourself. Your current situation is the result of your past decisions and previous choices. You are the only one with the power to change this if you want your life to be different or if you want to become a better person and advance with your life goals. Once you recognize this, you will be able to move forward without limits, knowing that you have the power within you. No one else will change your current situation, and it is completely up to you.

Changing Your Life through Positive Thinking

Everything that surrounds you in your life right now is the result of how you perceive life. Achieving better results and a better life depends on your determination to improve yourself and the perception you have about life. You need to be better in order to have a better life and you need to start thinking positively about life so your current situation starts to evolve and change.

It may be too basic, but it is the undeniable truth. If you want better results you need to make all the necessary adjustments to get those results. For instance, if you are a salesperson and want to have more sales, then you have to be proactive and make the necessary changes to become a better marketer and learn all the skills you need to have to get where you want to be. This works in the same way if you want to be a better father, a better student, or a better person. You need to change and reprogram your inner thoughts and be proactive always with a positive thinking mind. The world that surrounds you will never change unless you make the necessary changes inside your mind and transform your way of thinking.

Transform Your Life Perception

Once you change your inner thinking an entire new world will be unveiled through the magic of your new perception of life. To see and experience this magic in full action you will have to convince yourself that with a positive attitude towards everything in life, the quality of your life will also improve. In fact, once you start thinking differently and proactively about your life and about what you want to accomplish, you will be able to thrive because it is all about a change in attitude that will put you in an unstoppable path to success.

You have to overcome your fears, be proactive, and pursue what you know you can accomplish no matter what. If you want to be a better person or have better results in life then start making the necessary changes right now, not next week, not next month, right now! You know you deserve better, so start by changing you inner thinking and convince yourself that yes, you are capable of doing what you need to do to get where you want to be now. There is no limit on what you can accomplish once you change your mind. The only limit there is, is the self-inflicted blockage of negative thoughts and it is all inside you. You are the only one capable of controlling your thoughts; no one else is.

Remember, a positive thinking attitude requires action, don't be so naïve and expect that by just wishing things those things will come to you. They will definitely come to you once you combine the magic of positive thinking with unstoppable and proactive action. Know and define your goals so no matter what happens you always know where you are going even if you have to start all over again. This will reinforce your positive thinking attitude so the world that surrounds you starts to change in your favor with every step you take.

Always dream big and convince yourself that you can reach your dreams by taking the necessary steps to change your mindset from the inside out. By dreaming big, you stimulate your mind and new ideas and thoughts start to arise so your life starts to improve and you build up your self-esteem at the same time. Don't settle; always move forward and trust in yourself that you have the power to reach all of your dreams and succeed. You just have to change your mind and be always positive.

No matter what obstacles you may be experiencing in your life right now (financial, health, career, or relationship problems), you CAN turn things around with the magic of positive thinking.

POSITIVE THINKING IMAGES TO INSPIRE YOU

"Vision wihout action is a dream. Action without visión is simply passing the time. Action with VISION is making a positive difference." – Joal Barker

"Don't belive what your eyes are telling you. All they show is limitation.

Look with your understanding, find out what you already know, and you'll see the way to fly." – Richard Bach

"Nothing can stop the man with the right mental attitude from achieving his goal; Nothing on earth can help the man with the wrong mental attitude." – W.W. Ziege

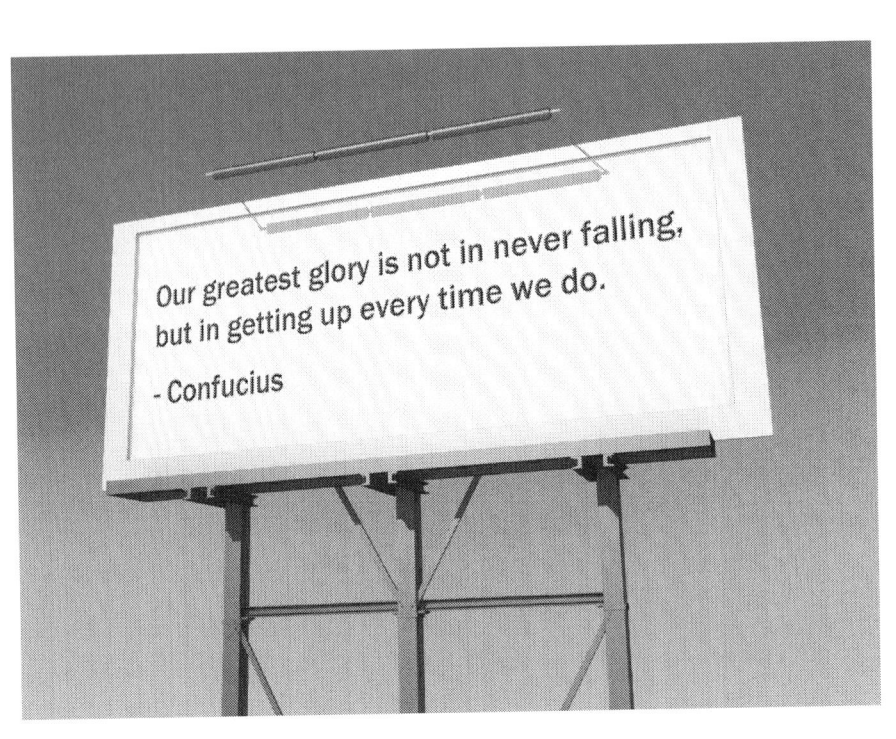

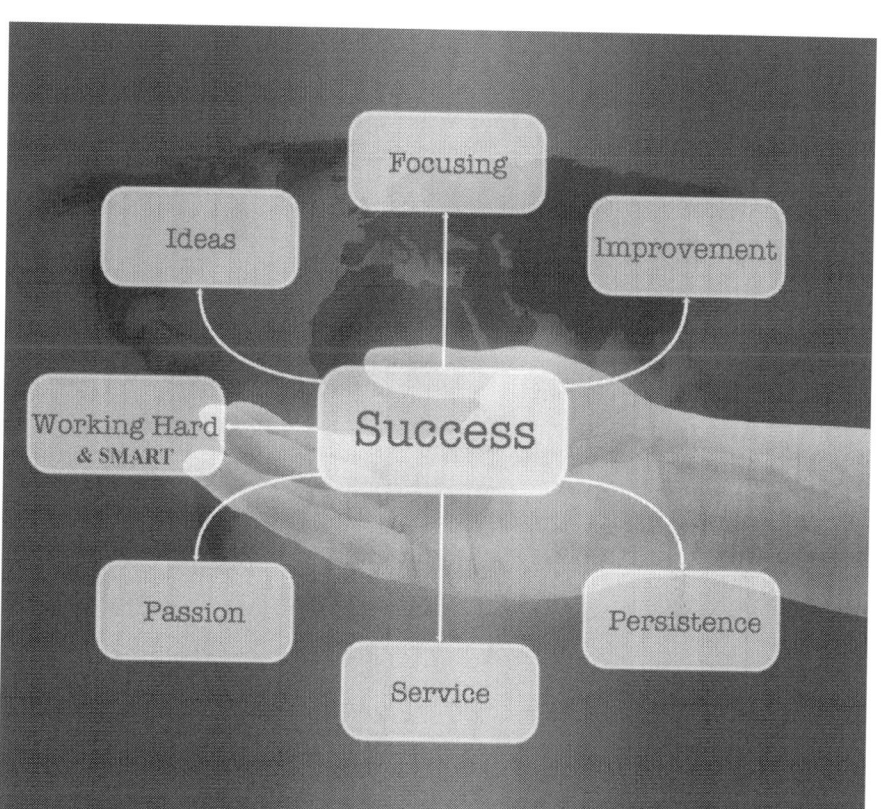

Positive Thinking and Motivational Quotes to Keep You Inspired

The following is a list of a wonderful selection of motivational and inspirational quotes that will help you find your inner strength and will feed your positive thinking mentality from now on. Never lose your enthusiasm and read these quote whenever you need inspiration and motivation to move forward with your goals.

"If opportunity doesn't knock, build a door." – Milton Berle

"Happiness often sneaks in through a door you didn't know you left open." – John Barrymore

"If you can change your mind, you can change your life." – William James

"The best way to gain self-confidence is to do what you are afraid to do." – Unknown

"You must make a decision that you are going to move on. It won't happen automatically. You will have to rise up and say, 'I don't care how hard this is, I don't care how disappointed I am, I'm not going to let this get the best of me. I'm moving on with my life." – Joel Osteen

"Success is falling nine times and getting up ten." – Jon Bon Jovi

"Whatever you want to do, do it now. There are only so many tomorrows." – Michael Landon

"I am the greatest, I said that even before I knew I was." – Muhammad Ali

"We are all here for some special reason. Stop being a prisoner of your past. Become the architect of your future." – Robin Sharma

"I do believe we're all connected. I do believe in positive energy. I do believe in the power of prayer. I do believe in putting good out into the world. And I believe in taking care of each other." - Harvey Fierstein

"I've had a lot of worries in my life, most of which never happened" – Mark Twain

"Life is a gift, and it offers us the privilege, opportunity, and responsibility to give something back by becoming more." – Tony Robbins

"The only place where your dream becomes impossible is in your own thinking." – Robert H Schuller

"Believe in yourself! Have faith in your abilities! Without a humble but reasonable confidence in your own powers you cannot be successful or happy." - Norman Vincent Peale

"Success is not a destination but the consciousness of knowing that you are enjoying what you are doing and by doing it every day you are rewarded with great results." - Frank Mullani

Having a Positive Thinking Mind – How It Can Benefit You

No doubt positive thinking is an amazing tool, but without taking action to adopt this attitude of mind, it is all just a waste of time. Being positive is a lifestyle more than just a fleeting moment of inspiration or a short-lived change of attitude towards life and towards the challenges you may encounter in your journey. It goes beyond just having a momentary positive thinking mind. Positive thinking can be regarded as a technique used to create positive affirmations that can counteract negative thoughts and doubts by neutralization and help to build your self-confidence which is essential to achieve all that you want in life. Both confidence and positive thinking go hand-in-hand to build your unstoppable winning attitude and your personality.

Thinking this way is a skill that can be learned and developed with constant practice, but is the habit of creating a positive thinking mind really worth the effort?

Being positive is not just having a naive and gullible attitude towards life, we cannot be convinced that only by the mere adoption of positive thought things will come our way without taking any action. Thinking in this way requires decisive action to see results. This is how the magic of positive thinking works by combining your strong positive attitude with action.

How do you define your own attitude towards life in the present moment?

How do you perceive life now, positively or negatively? It usually tends to be very easy to focus only on the negative aspects of life, especially if you do not have the tendency or mental training to see the bright side of things. But the reality is that it is just as easy to focus on the negative as it is to focus on the positive side of things, it all depends from which optic you want to look at things or the lens through which you perceive everything. The truth is that for every situation in life one has to take a perspective and according to the approach you decide to take will depend in a large percentage the result you get. The winner is the one who faces his challenges with strong positive approach, even in the most difficult situations of adversity because it transforms him in an even more persistent individual. Persistence is a characteristic of the person carrying positive thoughts as this goes hand in hand with building its confidence to achieve the results he want after persevering and insisting on a specific goal.

Conversely, the loser is the one who assumes an attitude of defeat even before he faces the problem or confronts what life puts ahead of him. Statements like: "I cannot do that; it is impossible" are the attitudes that destroy any possible progress. A positive person acts knowing that the challenge that lies ahead is probably something beyond their current capabilities but realizes that he is building success with every little step he takes and with every little victory achieved towards his lifetime goal. This attitude not only helps you travel the bumpy road that life is but also builds inner faith and strengthens your positive thinking personality.

When looking at the positive side, we can affect our subconscious minds and invoke the law of attraction. Then, we can attract a better set of circumstances in our lives. Remember to focus on the positive and always expect a positive result, even if this result is sometimes adverse, the positive mind learns from temporary defeats as these are experiences that become part of the arsenal that will give you the foundations to move forward.

There are two kinds of people: those who give up to a challenge, because their mental attitude predisposes them to an adverse outcome. Then, there are people that even in adversity are driven to move forward because they know that the result you seek is just a few more tries ahead. The most successful people in life do not give up because they are already winners having learned from their failures, they move ahead, they have a positive attitude and they learn from their mistakes. There is no such thing as a perfect human being or an invincible person, people who have achieved some success in life have attained it because they know that success is built with action and supported by a positive attitude. Did you know that it takes so much mental effort to think about the negative aspects of life as it takes to focus on the positive ones? It's all about attitude!

In a way, positive thinking is contagious and can lead to a "yes, I can" constant motto in an individual, team, or organization. It has been said that the only difference between success and failure is the mental attitude that the person has before facing a task.

Positive thinking is not improvised. This requires practice and should be your prevailing attitude towards life forever! Not sometimes, not just one day, but always! The very idea of convincing yourself that you're a positive person will help you feel safe or secure and move towards your goal. But remember the attitude alone just is not worth anything, you need to act. Action builds trust and reinforces and feeds this way of dealing with life.

Positive thinking is a mental attitude that gives entry to your mind to words and images that are favorable for your growth, for personal expansion and success. When you begin to develop a positive thinking mind you also develop a quality that allows you not only see the best in every situation, but that inevitably attracts the best results as a consequence of this new attitude towards life. You become a winner, not a loser with a simple change of attitude, you're in control of your mind and you can decide which approach you want to give to each situation.

What are the benefits? The funny thing with this change of attitude is that every time your results improve your self-esteem also grows and consequently your positive mindset gets stronger. Positive people are unstoppable, as each and every little last victory and goal achieved contribute to enlarge the winning personality they have. A positive person is a person who sees the best side of things even in adversity.

In history, there are many cases of people who have had personal misfortune to later transform that adversity into success. The truth is that many successful people have not had an easy road to accomplish their life dreams or they have not been given things on a silver platter. Abraham Lincoln is an example of a man who faced several defeats before going down in history as the character that unified a great nation and abolish slavery. He would certainly not have become president if after being defeated twice in his attempt to become a senator his persistence and positive thinking would not have prevailed. He failed in his first attempt to come to Congress and in his endeavor to be a businessman but he managed to achieve success with his tenacity and the power of positive thinking.

Thomas Edison was rated by his teachers as a "stupid" student that had difficulty to learn anything and was even expelled from his first two jobs for "incompetent." However before achieving success as an inventor he had over a thousand failed attempts before getting to finally make the light bulb work. When a reporter interviewed him after asking how he had so many failures, he replied: "these were not a thousand failures, they were a thousand steps that resulted in the invention of the light bulb." These are examples and models of positive thinking minds and persistence where the "failures" are simply a part of the process, never a total defeat for those who wait and insist until they get positive results. This is real evidence of real people who have achieved success through an unbreakable positive attitude. Through decisive action and tireless persistence they reached their life goals and this should be taken as inspiration for you and me to see that others have traveled through difficulties and bumpy roads showing us that the losers are those who give up before its time. Never give up; you know you are up to something when you define your lifetime goals.

It's in our hands and in our minds to choose a positive outlook towards life and overcome the attitude of defeat. We know that on the other side better outcomes are waiting for us for every situation, we just have to insist to let the power of the law of attraction unleash when we assume a winning and positive attitude. Faith and positive thinking are magical elements that give us the momentum we need and make us positive beings, what is the benefit? You get a better life in which you build a better way every day with success and positive results.

How to Eliminate Your Mental Blocks to Attain Success and be Positive

At some point in life we all feel stuck and paralyzed by diverse difficult situations like the lack of money, a complicated relationship, too much stress, a dead-end job or just the pure and disturbing fear of the unknown. But in reality what is stopping us from achieving success in life is our mental attitude.

We have a tendency to blame others for our own situation when the reality is that nothing around us will change unless we take control of our thoughts and take action. The only way to get better results is by addressing the mental blocks that are holding you hostage of your own mental made fears and excuses.

Reprogram your brain with positive self-affirmations

Your inner self talk is constantly sending messages from your subconscious mind to your conscious mind and these messages are ultimately controlling what you can and cannot do during your day. If your internal self-talk is negative you are preconditioning yourself for failure and defeat. This negative self-talk must be reprogramed in order to change your results and succeed throughout the day and throughout life. They way to reprogram your mind is through positive messages and affirmations that will rewrite your subconscious programing so you become a positive thinker and attract success and good results.

A great way to reprogram your brain with a new positive set of messages is by repetition. Each morning start the day by reading a list of **positive affirmations** (http://positivemental-attitude.blogspot.com/) that will ultimately convince your subconscious mind that you are a winner and you are capable of attaining everything that you want and you deserve it. This exercise of repetition must be a sort of ritual that you may want to practice each and every day during the day and before going to bed at night. Read every affirmation with faith and the conviction that what you are telling your mind by reading loudly is really possible and you will get it.

If fear of failure is one of your mental blocks, than replace your inner self-talk of "I am a failure" with "**I know I am a winner and I am capable to succeed and achieve my goals.**" The purpose of reading these types of positive self-talk loudly is to convince yourself that you really are who you think you are and by hearing it loudly your brain will accept the idea by repetition by taking action. To take action, stick to your plan, stick to your lifetime goals, and never stop dreaming and aiming for more by staying realistic at the same time.

By constantly doing this your brain will accept the new concepts and an indestructible and contagious positive attitude will start to develop inside you, and will become a part of you. Your old negative messages will be replaced by new and invigorating new ones that ultimately will affect your subconscious mind and defeat your mental blocks for good.

Expose your mind to a new set of positive messages. If your biggest concern and mental block is about money, then start by reading books that encourage you and show you the ways and methods of making more money. Start by watching new information in the form of videos, blogs, books and everything that will nourish and reprogram your mind with constructive new data and knowledge so you knock down your mental blocks about money. Scarcity and failure is a mind made blockage. The world is full of abundance, and you just have to know where to look and brainwash yourself with new positive ideas. You are what you think you are, but you also are what you consume. If you eat a lot then you most likely will become fat, if you consume positive content in the form of books, videos, etc… that transmits a positive and constructive message in relation to your goals and will definitely affect your mind in a positive way. So, stay away from negative messages and alarming news and focus all of your energy in achieving your goals and absorb all of the positive information you can from now on.

Another mental block we have is to think that we have enough time to pursue our goals. Keep in mind that we just need to manage our time and find the way to productively utilize the 24 hours that each day has. Plan your day every day. Know what your action plan will be and set aside some time you can dedicate to the pursuit of your lifetime goals. We have a tendency to waste time and to use our free time unproductively. We easily get immersed with distractions like instant messaging, TV, email, social web sites, etc… If you decide to dedicate at least the first hours of each day to focus your attention on activities that are in direct relation with your lifetime goals, you will definitely get good results. Wake up earlier or stay up later if necessary and by doing this every day you will soon discover that you are suddenly able to accomplish more and defeat the barrier and mental block of the lack of time.

Develop new Patterns and Change Your Environment

We have the ability to reset our minds once we change our surroundings. If your environment is full of clutter and disorganization this predisposes your mind for negative thoughts. On the contrary, if you have a neat and clean working environment your mind tends to clear and you will be more productive. Also try to connect with nature as often as you can to clear your mind and reset your brain. Sometimes we need to get out of the routine to restart with a refreshed positive attitude. Detox your mind and reserve a quiet time in connection with nature to reset both your inner being and your body. Sometimes our brains gets stuck in mental blocks and patterns that make it difficult for us to think clearly and positively, so don't forget to set some time aside periodically to refresh your brain by taking a holiday and reconnecting with nature. A simple walk in the park can be very refreshing and it is a great time to analyze your life goals or simply use it to relax your mind.

Conclusion:

I want to thank you for reading this book and I sincerely hope it has inspired you to move forward with your life and with the pursuit of your life goals. I honestly believe in the magic of positive thinking, I have experienced great results in my own personal life by applying this way of thinking each and every day of my life. We are all humans with our ups and downs and with tons of stress to manage and fears to overcome but I can tell you that we all have the power to succeed within our minds and we must always persevere to accomplish what we want from life. We are made from energy and positive energy definitely attracts more positive energy and certainly it attracts great outcomes in every endeavor we pursue in life.

One final thought, as much as we need to focus on our goals we also must enjoy the journey. This is crucial to keep our motivation; this is why it is so important to choose your lifetime goal according to what you really are passionate about so you can enjoy your journey towards your goals. **In fact success is not a destination but the consciousness of knowing that you are enjoying what you are doing and by doing it every day you are rewarded with great results.** Remember that persistence and action taking are the best friends of a positive thinking mindset to achieve all you want in life. My honest desire is that you accomplish all of your dreams in life through the magic of positive thinking. THANK YOU FOR READING MY BOOK! AND ALWAYS BELIEVE IN YOU! YES YOU CAN ACHIEVE ALL YOU WANT AND BE POSITIVE!

Please leave a Positive Review if you liked this book and if you think it helped you get inspired here:

http://tinyurl.com/positive-thinking-book

Get a **FREE** copy of the Best **Positive Affirmations** NOW! Here:

http://positivemental-attitude.blogspot.com/

Other books by Frank Mullani: http://tinyurl.com/the-magic-of-motivation

Dedication:

I dedicate this book to my two sons, to my family and to you with the hope that it will help you get where you want to be, thank you once again for reading this book.

About the Author:

Frank Mullani is a self-made author who strongly believes in creating your own opportunities through the power of positive thinking and persistence. He has experienced countless ups and downs throughout his life facing a lot of adversity but always prevailing and conquering life through the magic of positive thinking, a strong motivation and his resilience. After literally losing it all, Frank is now back on his feet and finding success by strongly embracing one of his most valuable assets, his positive thinking mind.

His goal is to transmit his encouraging way of thinking to as many people as possible through his books. He strongly believes that every one deserves success and that we humans are capable

of attaining everything we want in life by applying the magic of positive thinking, a strong motivation and persistence, and that is the main message that he wants to send to his readers.

Legal Disclaimer

This book is designed to provide information and motivation to readers. It is sold with the understanding that the publisher is not engaged to the reader in any type of psychological, legal, or other kind of professional advice. The content of each chapter is the sole expression and opinion of its author, and not necessarily that of the publisher. No warranties or guarantees are expressed or implied by the publisher's choice to include any of the content in this volume. Neither the publisher nor the individual author of this book shall be liable for any physical, psychological, emotional, financial, or commercial damages, including, but not limited to, special, incidental, consequential or other damages. Our views and rights are the same: You are responsible for your own choices, actions and results.

Made in the USA
Lexington, KY
01 December 2014